Hawthorne & History

Defacing It.

J. Hillis Miller

Basil Blackwell

First published 1991

Basil Blackwell, Inc.
3 Cambridge Center
Cambridge, Massachusetts 02142, USA

Basil Blackwell Ltd
108 Cowley Road, Oxford, OX4 1JF, UK

Library of Congress Cataloging in Publication Data
Miller, J. Hillis (Joseph Hillis), 1928–
    Hawthorne and history : defacing it / J. Hillis Miller.
      p.   cm. — (The Bucknell lectures in literary theory)
    Includes bibliographical references and index.
    ISBN 0–631–17559–8   — ISBN 0–631–17561–X (pbk.)
    1. Hawthorne, Nathaniel, 1804–1864—Criticism and interpretation.
  I. Title.   II. Series
  PS1888.M55   1990   90–39667
  813'.3—dc20   CIP

British Library Cataloguing in Publication Data
A CIP catalogue record for this book is available from the British Library.

Typeset in 11 on 13 pt Plantin
by Photo·graphics, Honiton, Devon
Printed in Great Britain by Billing & Sons Ltd, Worcester

Contents

Preface

Fundamental and far-reaching changes in literary studies, often compared to paradigmatic shifts in the sciences, have been taking place during the last thirty years. These changes have included enlarging the literary canon not only to include novels, poems, and plays by writers whose race, gender, or nationality had marginalized their work, but also to include texts by philosophers, psychoanalysts, historians, anthropologists, social and religious thinkers, who previously were studied by critics merely as "background". The stance of the critic and student of literature is also now more in question than ever before. In 1951 it was possible for Cleanth Brooks to declare with confidence that the critic's job was to describe and evaluate literary objects, implying the relevance for criticism of the model of scientific objectivity while leaving unasked questions concerning significant issues in scientific theory, such as complementarity, indeterminacy, and the use of metaphor. Now the possibility of value-free skepticism is itself in doubt as many feminist, Marxist, and psychoanalytic theorists have stressed the inescapability of ideology and the consequent obligation of teachers and students of litertaure to declare their political, axiological, and aesthetic positions in order to make those positions conscious and available for examination. Such expansion and deepening of literary studies has, for many critics, revitalized their field.

Those for whom the theoretical revolution has been regenerative would readily echo, and apply to criticism, Lacan's call to revitalize psychoanalysis: "I consider it to be an urgent task to disengage from concepts that are being deadened by routine use the meaning that they regain both from a re-examination of their history and from a reflexion on their subjective foundations. That, no doubt, is the teacher's prime function."

Many practising writers and teachers of literature, however, see recent developments in literary theory as dangerous and anti-humanistic. They would insist that displacement of the centrality of the word, claims for the "death of the author", emphasis upon gaps and incapacities in language, and indiscriminate opening of the canon threaten to marginalize literature itself. In this view the advance of theory is possible only because of literature's retreat in the face of aggressive moves by Marxism, feminism, deconstruction, and psychoanalysis. Furthermore, at a time of militant conservatism and the dominance of corporate values in America and Western Europe, literary theory threatens to diminish further the declining audience for literature and criticism. Theoretical books are difficult to read; they usually assume that their readers possess knowledge that few have who have received a traditional literary education; they often require massive reassessments of language, meaning, and the world; they seem to draw their life from suspect branches of other disciplines: professional philosophers usually avoid Derrida; psychoanalysts dismiss Freud as unscientific; Lacan was excommunicated by the International Psycho-Analytical Association.

The volumes in this series record part of the attempt at Bucknell University to sustain conversation about changes in literary studies, the impact of those changes on literary art, and the significance of literary theory for the humanities and human sciences. A generous grant from the Andrew W. Mellon Foundation has made possible a five-year series of visiting lectureships by internationally-known participants in the reshaping of literary studies. Each volume includes a comprehensive introduction to the published work of the lecturer, the Bucknell Lectures, an interview, and a comprehensive bibliography.

The editors would like to express their gratitude to the participants in the faculty seminars on literary theory, particularly to Pauline Fletcher, for their unfailing support of this project. We would also like to thank Barbara Cohen, Holly Henry, and Brenda O'Boyle for their invaluable work on the bibliography.

Introduction

Mere reading, it turns out, prior to any theory, is able to transform critical discourse in a manner that would appear deeply subversive to those who think of the teaching of literature as a substitute for the teaching of theology, ethics, psychology, or intellectual history.

Paul de Man, "The Return to Philology"

For philology is that venerable art which demands of its votaries one thing above all: to go aside, to take time, to become still, to become slow – it is a goldsmith's art and connoisseurship of the *word* which has nothing but delicate, cautious work to do and achieves nothing if it does not achieve it *lento* . . . . This art does not so easily get anything done, it teaches to read *well*, that is to say, to read slowly, deeply, looking cautiously before and aft, with reservations, with doors left open, with delicate eyes and fingers.[1]

Friedrich Nietzsche, *Daybreak*

J. Hillis Miller has decisively shaped the landscape of modern American literary criticism. Originally a physics major at Oberlin College, Miller turned to literature after two years, and received his Ph.D. from Harvard in 1952. A prolific writer, he has published eight books (with at least two more due shortly) and has written some one hundred articles, as well as numerous reviews and introductions. He is associated, as editor or member of the advisory

Board, with numerous journals, among them *Modern Language Notes*, *Victorian Studies*, *Dickens Studies*, *ELH*, *PMLA*, *Diacritics*, *The Georgia Review*, *PTL*, *Genre*, *Studies in English Literature*, *Oxford Literary Review*, and *Poetics Today*. His career, accordingly, reflects the major stances of American literary criticism of the past thirty years.

In its self-declared search for formal unity of Dickensian imagery, Miller's long and carefully documented dissertation, *Dickens' Symbolic Imagery: A Study of Six Novels*, is an exploration of Kenneth Burke's notion of symbolic action. Miller's concerns are not solely formalistic; the unity of imaginative vision in a novel serves a larger purpose: "In successful imaginative discourse the sense of life is not simply something known conceptually with the mind but is also something experienced, as the real world is experienced" (DSI, p.x). Miller's interest in the "sense of the world" throughout the book is an early indication of the direction which his critical outlook took after his assignment as Assistant Professor at Johns Hopkins in 1953. There his friendship with Georges Poulet brought about a change that has had a lasting impact on critical attitudes in the United States.[2]

With Poulet as his *spiritus rector*, Miller completely revised his dissertation and published it in 1959 as *Charles Dickens: The World of His Novels*. His concern with the relationship between "an imagining mind and its objects" is here his basic presupposition, and the center of the literary work is no longer a central symbol or a key metaphor or a commanding image from which all the imagery radiates, but the mind of the author: "Taken all together, all the unit passages form the imaginative universe of the writer. Through the analysis of all the passages, as they reveal the persistence of certain obsessions, problems, and attitudes, the critic can hope to glimpse the original unity of a creative mind. For all the works of a single writer form a unity, a unity in which a thousand paths radiate from the same center" (CD, p. ix). This concern with the exploration of the author's *cogito* soon establishes Miller's role as the foremost American "critic of consciousness".

Hillis Miller's next two books, *The Disappearance of God* (1963) and *Poets of Reality* (1965) represent both a refinement and a substantial expansion of the phenomenological approach professed in *Charles Dickens*. While the latter focuses on the atmosphere created by the consciousness of one single author, *The Disappearance of God* examines five nineteenth-century writers (De Quincey, Browning, Emily Brontë, Arnold, Hopkins) and relates them to each other and to the Victorian *Zeitgeist*. Miller argues that "the comprehension of literature takes place through a constant narrowing and expansion of the focus of attention, from the single work of an author, to the whole body of his works, to the spirit of the age, and back again in a contraction and dilation which is the living motion of interpretation" (DG, p. 12). At the same time Miller contends in his excellent introduction that these five writers epitomize the telophase of a long process of man's gradual disconnection from God. While the majority of the romantic poets take for granted the presence of a hidden spiritual force in nature, for the writers Miller discusses this is no longer true. They situate the spiritual power beyond the world rather than in the world. Still, these Victorians attempt to bring God back to this world in order to "recover immanence in a world of transcendence" (DG, p. 15).

Poets of Reality is in many ways a continuation of *The Disappearance of God*. Miller's argument again hinges on the consequence of God's displacement. Yet, in contrast to their predecessors, the "poets of reality" do not interpret God's invisibility as a result of his presence beyond the world but rather of his nonexistence. "If the disappearance of God is presupposed by much Victorian poetry, the death of God is the starting point for many twentieth-century writers" (PR, p. 2). Miller understands the death of God for these writers as a mere logical consequence of Cartesianism followed to its extremes: through man's definition of the ego as subject, everything else is turned into object, and God thus becomes a mere object of thought. At this point the thinking subject becomes a nihilist. Nihilism is looming large in our culture, but if it is exposed as what it is, it is possible to transcend it by understanding it. This is the particular achievement of Joseph Conrad. His thorough exploration of the depths of nihilism opens up a pathway past it. Consequently, Miller's book begins with a chapter on Conrad and then proceeds to a close observation of the different attempts by five twentieth-century writers, Yeats, Eliot, Thomas, Stevens, and Williams to pass on from nihilism to a new reality.

The Disappearance of God and Poets of Reality signal more than the widening of Miller's critical scope. They mark the shift to a new critical target. The Dickens study is a quest for the constitutive unity at the center of the universe formed by that author's writing. Both The Disappearance of God and Poets of Reality lead one step beyond this goal in that they are quests of quests. In these books, Miller is trying to account for the primum mobile behind, and common to, the shaping force of each individual literary universe. The identification of each author's consciousness is still Miller's aim, but it now serves an ancillary function. The goal now is the identification of the center that organizes the various centers. And Miller's answer is that it is the quest for a God who has become increasingly more difficult to find since the end of the middle ages.

The significance of the Pouletian phase of Miller's critical career for American literary criticism can hardly be overestimated. Miller introduced criticism of consciousness in his 1963 essay on Poulet ("The Literary Criticism of George Poulet", Modern Language Notes) and three years later in "The Geneva School: The Criticism of Marcel Raymond, Albert Béguin, Georges Poulet, Jean Rousset, Jean-Pierre Richard, and Jean Starobinski" (The Critical Quarterly). His writings sensitized American literary critics to continental modes of thinking in general – attitudes, modes of thinking that had hitherto received attention at best in the philosophy, German, or French departments of universities. Familiarity with Kierkegaard, Nietzsche, Husserl, Heidegger, Merleau-Ponty, Sartre, and Bachelard was soon essential for the reception of "literary" existentialism in the United States.

Two factors are responsible for Miller's success: his role as a mediator and the attractiveness of his critical method. His ability to locate and extract essentials of European thinking made these virtually untapped resources available to a broader range of Anglo-American critics. On the other hand, his critical method combines a formalism, which is sufficient to make it palatable to a critical scene largely trained in New Criticism, with a new method capable of replacing both a New Criticism that had grown stale and an archetypal criticism whose aestheticist coercions had been recognized as problematical.

In 1969 Miller published a small volume entitled *The Form of Victorian Fiction*. The study focuses on six major Victorian novelists: Thackeray, Dickens, Trollope, George Eliot, Meredith, and Hardy. It explores the role and function of time as a fundamental dimension of fiction, the constitutive significance of interpersonal relations (Gabriel Marcel's "intersubjectivity"), and notably the relation between language and reality. In spite of its brevity, this book indicates a significant shift of critical attention away from the individual authorial consciousness to a "transindividual mind", which ultimately embraces the thinking of the Victorian novelists and critics. Miller's contention that the "Victorian novelist tends to assume that each man finds himself from his birth surrounded by a transindividual mind, identical with the words he learns" (FVF, p. 67) echoes Poulet "conscience commune à tous les esprits contemporains", as does his deflation of language's claim to be referential or to represent a separate reality, and it anticipates fundamental claims later labeled as post-structuralist:

The play of reality within reality in a novel, of narrator within narrator, of language within language, leads ultimately, however, to the revelation that both sides of the looking glass are the same. Human culture and the imitation of human culture in a novel have the same substance and the same structure. *Both have the nature of language.* (FVF, p. 140, italics added)

Many of Miller's more recent critical notions are already present in his Geneva criticism. With his adoption of Pouletian strategies of "involvement" instead of aesthetic distance (what Fish calls "courting the affective fallacy") he has forsaken any New-Critical stance of aloofness, and is coming to see himself as being inside what he will later describe as a labyrinth, in which the text and the critic are trapped alike. Another basic tenet, that the critic's fate is inextricably chained to that of the text he interprets, to a degree where the two become mere versions of each other, is expressed in his description of the attitude in which the critic regards himself as producing *literature about literature*. This is one of the common denominators of the Geneva critics. As a critic of consciousness, Miller pays attention not merely to the individual work but rather to the entire canon of a particular writer. With this, a note or a diary, a fragment, or a letter is no longer ranked inferior beforehand, or ancillary, but potentially equal to a poem or an entire novel in its capability of revealing the mind of its creator. This shift of focus from the individual, well-defined, self-contained work of art to the consideration of the entirety of an artist's output as a continuum consisting of self-similar links marks a major re-assessment of the functional value of traditional literary categories and foreshadows an important deconstructionist doctrine.

His fourth book, *Thomas Hardy: Distance and Desire* (1970), is not only an outstanding piece of Hardy criticism but follows up Miller's gradual transition from phenomenology to post-structuralism. Although he begins with a pledge of faith to his formerly professed criticism of consciousness, and although the book is still Genevan in its collocation of widely dispersed passages and its moving back and forth between novels and lyric poetry, the preface tells us that strong undercurrents are at work in this book. What had been a major *desideratum* of Geneva criticism, namely that the critic's consciousness be informed as extensively as possible by the author's consciousness present in his writing, is now declared to be an ineluctable ruse of language. There is no such thing, Miller claims, as an extra-linguistic origin that enables the critic to rise above the literary work and assume a position of objective detachment. Both critic and text are entrammeled in the same labyrinth from which there is no escape. This strong echo of Derrida's "il n"y a rien hors du texte" not only topples the throne of critical privilege, but also brings about an utterly different attitude towards terms like "reality", "history", or "source". These concepts are false friends promising a stable and reliable point of reference from which a given text can be surveyed in interpretive stability. What is erroneously assumed to be a reliable point of reference is merely another sign:

> The relation of a novel to its sources is not that of a sign to a referent which is unequivocally factual, but that of one sign to another sign, one human meaning to another human meaning. The facts of Hardy's life or of nineteenth-century European history are not physical objects. They are human significances, interpretations which are themselves in need of interpretation. They can only be interpreted in terms of other significances which are anterior to them, and those anterior ones to others more anterior still so that a true beginning or source can never be reached. (TH, p. 36)

In the long interval between the publication of the book on Thomas Hardy and his next book *Fiction and Repetition* in 1982, Miller published – among almost three dozen

essays – a number of often-quoted seminal articles elucidat-
ing the position of a deconstructionist literary critic.
"Geneva or Paris? The Recent Work of Georges Poulet"
(1970), is an attempt at reconciling Poulet with Derrida
that turns out to be a subtle and reverential deconstruction.
The article thus testifies both to the extent to which Derrida's influence had developed since his Johns Hopkins début
in 1966 and to the anxiousness the transition created in
Miller. Miller claims that Poulet's criticism ultimately lays
bare its own foundations and concerns itself with the same
"problematical issues" that are cardinal for a critic like
Derrida. Although Poulet has no desire, Miller explains,
to "deconstruct" metaphysics, his encounter with the instability of the auctorial cogito has already done that for him:
"Poulet's exploration of the *Cogito* of each of his writers
leads to the recognition that the *Cogito* is the experience of
a lack of a beginning, of an irremediable instability of the
mind" (GP, pp. 223–4).

A much more outspoken critique of a critic and a much
more distinct statement of deconstructive attitudes (a few
don'ts by a deconstructionist, so to speak) appeared in 1975
in *Diacritics* under the title "Deconstructing the Deconstructors". This review of Joseph Riddel's *The Inverted
Bell*, a book on William Carlos Williams, is a tough, but
very perceptive and important model for deconstructive
analysis, and, particularly in the final pages, an explicit
addressing of a number of putative misconceptions about
the operation of deconstruction. One of the things Miller
finds wanting in Riddel's book is a treatment of the 'linguistic moment", "the moment of criticism which hovers in a
prolonged interrogation of language as such" (DD, p. 29).
What he regards as most problematic, however, is Riddel's
failure "to recognize consistently the necessary heterogeneity of any text" (DD, p. 30). An inevitable consequence
of this is the fact that the deconstructive discourse itself
"can never reach a clarity which is not vulnerable to being
deconstructed in its turn" (DD, p. 30). The critical text,

like the text it criticizes, is merely a link in a chain, for it is open to criticism, and its criticism can be dismantled, and so on. In the same way that Miller shows Riddel's work to be incoherent, he adds, Rousseau may be "deconstructed" by Derrida, who may in turn be dismounted by de Man, who . . . , etc.:

> The heterogeneity of a text (and so its vulnerability to deconstruction) lies . . . in the fact that it says two entirely incompatible things at the same time. Or rather, it says something which is capable of being interpreted in two irreconcilable ways. It is "undecidable". One way is referential (there is an origin), and the other the deconstruction of this referentiality (there is no origin, only the freeplay of linguistic substitution). The deconstruction, however, is necessarily formulated in such a way that it can be taken as referential in its turn, or else it would not be able to perform its act of deconstruction. But the deconstruction has been undertaken in order to deny the referentiality of the language in question. Aporia, impasse, *malconfort*, in which one can neither sit nor stand. (DD, p. 30)

Miller insists, nonetheless, that all impasses of deconstruction are not equal, as they may differ in their degree of self-awareness. Besides, he claims (and here we find one of the few blatant inconsistencies in his writing), the chain of deconstruction is not an infinite one but leads to "a gradual clarification" via a reiterated encounter of the "same" aporia. However, how this clarification is to be gained (and, most important of all, how the reader may be sure that it is clarification rather than confusion) is – *nil mirar* – never stated.

It is of crucial importance, Miller points out in the final paragraphs, to realize that the dismantling of the text is not performed from the outside by a critic, rather "the 'unreadability' (if there is such a word) of a text is more than an experience of unease in the reader, the result of his failure to reduce the text to a homogeneous reading . . . The text performs on itself the act of deconstruction without any help from the critic. The text expresses its own aporia . . . " (DD, p. 31). Yet, although this outlook radically redefines the role of the critic (he is no longer the "origin", but merely the witness bound to report what has always already taken place), Miller does not dwell on the consequences of this re-allocation of authority.

The long two-part essay, "Stevens" Rock and Criticism as Cure" (1976) exhibits clear traces of Derrida's "White Mythology". The significance of Miller's essay lies in its introduction and perspicuous practical application in literary criticism of particular deconstructionist (primarily Derridian) key terms and attitudes. The first part, a deconstructive reading of Wallace Stevens' "The Rock", exemplifies Derrida's notion of semantic *dissémination*. An etymon, Miller demonstrates, is incapable of providing one single, homogeneous, and stable meaning for a given word. On the contrary: etymology reveals the simultaneous presence of several conflicting meanings, leading the searcher only deeper into the impenetrable thicket of words. To illuminate the implications of this impasse, Miller has recourse to Derrida's *mise en abyme* (with an account of its own labyrinthine etymology) and uses it as an angle of attack for a reading of "The Rock". Towards the end of the first part, the critical scope transcends the realm of the poem to include basic tenets of Western thought. Drawing heavily on the concept of *catachresis*, Miller repeatedly denies the validity of a distinction between literal and figurative. "The fiction of the literal or proper", he declares, "is therefore the supreme fiction. All poetry and all language are *mises en abyme*, since all language is based on catachresis."[3]

In the often reprinted second half of the essay Miller examines what appear to be two mutually exclusive attitudes towards literature. Echoing the Freudian *heimlich-unheimlich* he distinguishes "canny" from "uncanny" critics. The former presume the existence of "solid advances", frequently regard themselves as "scientists", and thus believe in the omnipotence of thinking and its ability to (Miller quotes Nietzsche) "penetrate the deepest abysses of being". The latter, on the other hand, the "uncanny" critics (identified, among others, as the Yale School with the inclusion of Derrida), realize that all of their investigations will always reach a point where their procedure ceases to make "rational sense" and aporia looms large. The distinction between the two camps gradually vaporizes in the course of the essay until it becomes clear that it is untenable. The canny becomes uncanny and the uncanny is in perpetual danger of becoming canny. That is why the uncanny critics must – in the teeth of the inevitable reversal canny-uncanny-canny – beware of terminological petrification which might lead to mechanical application of deconstructive discourse. The end of the essay with its wryly ambiguous formulation of the tasks of criticism in the immediate future as the "exploration" "of this coming and going in quest [!] and in questioning of the ground", however betrays *les traces* of Miller's secret yearning for the ground he has just appeared to have blasted to pieces so thoroughly.

In an influential essay that proclaims the extensive further absorption of cardinal post-structuralist attitudes, Miller treats more in depth an axiomatic conception he had touched upon in his Hardy book: the notion of the inescapable labyrinth of language which precludes the critic from effecting an "outside" approach to the text. "Ariadne's Thread: Repetition and the Narrative Line" (1976) examines the limits of criticism. Miller demonstrates how it is impossible for any narrative terminology to escape the entanglements of the metaphor of the "line". In view of any traditional terminology that makes use of the "line" this means that the relationship of meaning is never one between sign and thing, but always, and insurmountably so, one between sign and sign. As a result, the critic explodes by his very investigation the difference between figurative and literal language, between text and reality, between starting-point and a repetition of it, between what the author says and what the narrator. His own exploration is no exception, Miller hastens to add, it is subject to the same coercions and consequently "to be defined as an impossible search for the center of the maze, the Minotaur or spider which has created and so commands it all" (AT, p. 72).

This denial of the existence of what logocentric metaphysics would call "center", or "origin", is further exemplified in Miller's penetrating yet very accessible deconstruction of a passage from *Troilus and Cressida* published under the title "Ariachne's Broken Woof" (1977). After a brief examination of the various explanations that have been ventured for a monological interpretation of Shakespeare's enigmatic *Ariachne*, he dismisses them all in favor of a dialogical, quasi-portmanteau reading (*Ariadne* + *Arachne* = *Ariachne*), crediting I. A. Richards with "breaking through the ponderous weight of metaphysical prejudice" (ABW, p. 46). One after the other, basic logocentric key terms like "unity" "authority", (and with it "author") "cause", "reason" are radically called in question. All of them are fundamentally heterogeneous, Miller argues, following Derrida, in that they contain both logocentric metaphysics and its subversion at the same time. The tracking of such heterogeneity is not the principal goal of deconstructive criticism, however, he cautions:

"Deconstruction" as a procedure of interpreting the texts of our tradition is not simply a teasing out of the traces of that dialogical heterogeneity. The danger of heterogeneity has been traditionally recognized, as, for example, Plato recognized and attempted to reduce the threat posed by the Sophists. Deconstruction rather attempts to reverse the implicit hierarchy within the terms in which the dialogical has been defined. It attempts to define the monological, the logocentric, as a derived effect of the dialogical rather than as the noble affirmation of which the dialogical is a disturbance, a secondary shadow in the originating light. Deconstruction attempts a crisscross substitution of early and late and a consequent vibratory displacement of the whole system of Western metaphysics. (ABW, p. 59–60)

Miller concludes his essay by calling attention to the eternal plight of the deconstructive critic: he himself is forced to use the very rhetoric of metaphysics that he is out to dismantle in his act of deconstruction. The deconstructive critic must carry on – in full awareness of the inevitability of his failure – and continue to fight the windmills of the text.

Another milestone, picking up where "Ariachne's Broken Woof" has left off – with the image of the relation of parasite and host – is "The Critic as Host" (1977). This refutation of M. H. Abrams' charges that deconstructionist reading is "plainly and simply parasitical" is a refulgent display of the pervasiveness of the mechanisms that deconstruction aims at laying bare. In the course of Miller's skilful etymological investigation of the "meaning" of the word "parasite" it becomes apparent that the putative simple polarity between "guest" and "host" is untenable. Both words, he argues, are interlocked so intricately that they cannot be used unequivocally. A host, it turns out, is a guest, and a guest a host. Thus the parasite is always already present in the host. In the light of his investigation "[each] word in itself becomes separated by the strange logic of the "para", membrane which divides inside from outside and yet joins them in a hymeneal bond, or allows an osmotic mixing, making the strangers friends, the distant near, the dissimilar similar, the *unheimlich heimlich*, the homely homey, without, for all its closeness and similarity, ceasing to be strange, distant, dissimilar" (CH, p. 443). With this, Abrams' claim is elegantly inserted in a directionless chain where his reading might with equal right be called the parasite, and the deconstructionist reading the host. The scope of the essay surpasses that of mere rebuttal, though, and becomes an excellent example of deconstructive strategy at work. Miller insists that the unexpected reversal of positions is by no means the establishment of a new hierarchy in which deconstruction yields true or "univocal" meaning as opposed to traditional reading. Much rather, deconstruction uncovers the inherent undecidability of readings: "Each contains, necessarily, its enemy within itself, is itself both host and parasite" (CH, p. 447). This point is made very clear again in Miller's 1979 assessment of the state of the (then) more recent tendencies in American criticism ("On Edge: The Crossways of Literary Criticism"):

> An antimetaphysical or "deconstructive" form of literary study attempts to show that in a given work of literature, in a different way in each case, metaphysical assumptions are both present and at the same time undermined by the text itself. They are undermined by some figurative play within the text which forbids it to be read as an "organic unity" organized around some version of the logos . . . The following out of the implications of the play of tropes leads to a suspension of fully rationalizable meaning in the experience of an aporia or boggling of the mind.[4]

This denial of the validity of the axiom of non-contradiction (A cannot be A and not-A at the same time) is the main line of argument of Miller's *Fiction and Repetition* (1982), a study that traces the simultaneous presence of two mutually exclusive forms of repetition in seven nineteenth and twentieth-century novels. It appears in the form of the grounded and the ungrounded repetitive chain. Referring to a distinction made by Gilles Deleuze in *Logique du sens*, Miller explains that the former ("Platonic") conception is based on an invariable archetype which acts as a model for all other examples. This is the basic model behind realistic

fiction. The latter ("Nietzschean") notion of repetition postulates the insurmountable difference between things: no
two things are alike and any impression of similarity or
even identity between them is unfounded – a mere result
of their differential interrelation. In all the novels discussed
in *Fiction and Repetition*, Miller finds both forms of repetition to be present at the same time, although they appear
logically to exclude each other. This violation of the either/
or axiom, he emphasizes, is "a working principle of deconstruction" (FR, p. 17).

As unsettling as Miller's assertive premise might appear,
the critical practice professed in *Fiction and Repetition* is
much less disturbing. While there is no longer a stable,
unified meaning or a number of such meanings waiting
for deliverance like the Frog Prince, an interpretation,
particularly of motives and themes, is still possible and
sensible:

> Taken together, the elements form a system of mutually
> defining motifs, each of which exists as its relation to
> the others. The reader must execute a lateral dance of
> interpretation to explicate any given passage, without ever
> reaching, in this sideways movement, a passage which is
> chief, original, or originating, a sovereign principle of expla-
> nation. The meaning, rather, is suspended within the inter-
> action among the elements. It is immanent rather than
> transcendent. This does not mean that one interpretation
> is as good as another but that the meaning must be formu-
> lated not as a hierarchy, with some *ur*-explanation at the
> top, truest of the true, but as an interplay among a definable
> and limited set of possibilities, all of which have force, but
> all of which may not logically have force at once. (FR,
> p. 127)

Fiction and Repetition demonstrates how Miller's deconstruction is very much a criticism *sui generis*. Despite the
battle-cries of his adversaries, Miller's criticism does not

bring about the end of humanism nor the subversion or loss of "values" (literary and metaphysical). It is true that in his post-1970 work he systematically catechizes the unquestioned acceptance of what have long been believed to be stable entities, the "meaning" or "extent" of a given text, the "self" of an author. But he does not simply discard such concepts. Miller is a moderate deconstructionist. His criticism subtly emphasizes the fundamental deconstructive tenet that the "traditional" or "metaphysical" elements are coexistent (or rather inextricably intertwined) with the concepts denying their very *raison d'être*. While they lead a different kind of existence, a sort of hybrid between presence and absence, they never vanish altogether. Similarly, claims that his criticism advocates the unsustainability of reproducible statements about literature or the futility of critical analysis are untenable. In *Fiction and Repetition* Miller states unmistakably that "[t]he emotional experience of following through the novel no doubt forms that background of agreement about the novel which is shared by almost all readers and forms the basis for discussions of it and even for disagreements about what the novel means" (FR, p. 119). Miller does not even interfere with the traditional literary canon: *Lord Jim, Wuthering Heights, Henry Esmond, Tess of the d'Urbervilles, The Well-Beloved, Mrs Dalloway,* and *Between the Acts,* like most other of Miller's topics, are among the *pièces de résistance* of the reading lists of most universities and colleges.

Although often causing varying degrees of discomfort ranging from the refreshing to the unsettling, the results of J. Hillis Miller's criticism do not subvert fundamental givens of traditional literary criticism. Nineteen years at Johns Hopkins have left their traces on him as has the influence of Georges Poulet, Earl Wassermann and Kenneth Burke. Miller's intelligent, sensitive interpretations – testifying to a remarkably wide reading – are only very rarely elusive (notably when he is reading after Freud and

Lacan). They are refreshing as well as admirable in their dexterous application of difficult philosophical conceptions. But their ultimate goal is conventional:

> It seemed to me when I began the study of literature, as it still seems to me now, that one of the most obvious characteristics of works of literature is their manifest strangeness as integuments of words. Poets, novelists, and playwrights say things which are exceedingly odd by most everyday standards of normality. Any way of interpreting literature would need to account for that oddness. (FR, p. 18)

One of Miller's strongest motivations in *Fiction and Repetition* is "to devise a way to remain aware of the strangeness of the language of literature and to try to account for it" (FR, p. 21). We have it on Miller's testimony that for him Poulet's particular appeal lay in the ability of his theories to solve the problem of the lost unifying whole. The possibility of reconstructing an author's consciousness in turn enabled him to account for the most divergent and seemingly incompatible features of a specific author's writing. As a deconstructionist, his motivation is, interestingly enough, largely unchanged. Does not "totality" and "the total reading of the work" echo the "lost unifying whole"?

> One characteristic of my own criticism is a desire to account for the totality of a given work, a desire which, insofar as it is not simply constitutional, is probably an inheritance from the New Criticism. Certainly it is possible to be satisfied with a partial or approximate reading of a given work. Many good critical essays stop short of claiming to account for the whole, though most indicate at least implicitly what such an accounting would be like. My training has led me to presuppose that the best critical essays are those which more or less overtly confront the

question of what a total reading of the work at hand would be. (FR, pp. 17–8)

In *The Linguistic Moment* (1985), the focus is again on reading, not on theorizing. And once more Miller's dislike for a "rarefied atmosphere of pure theory" permeates these pages. Still, the starting point is a theoretical conception – that of the "linguistic moment". Miller defines it as the moment in which the texts of poems become self-reflexive, exploding the tacit assumption that language can be a transparent medium of meaning whenever it sets out to do so. In addition, Miller argues, in the poetry he examines three radically different theories of poetry are caught up in a never-ending conflict that permeates all Western languages: poetry as mimesis, poetry as an act (the mind seeking revelation in and through the words), and poetry as creation (as opposed to discovery). He demonstrates that whenever language becomes problematic in Wallace Stevens' poetry, a rapid interplay between these theories begins which prevents any of them being singled out as a stable point of reference. As *The Linguistic Moment* is meant to be a "testing of the grounds for or of" the poems it discusses, it is set somewhere in between theory and practice, it is a critique, Miller insists. Each of the chapters on Wordsworth, Shelley, Browning, Hopkins, Hardy, Yeats, Williams, and Stevens is in its own way probing for ground. All of them come to the same conclusion as the last, the model chapter (a revised version of his earlier "Stevens' Rock and Criticism as Cure"): there is no solid ground.

Stevens' poem is an abyss and the filling of the abyss, a chasm and a production of icons of the chasm. Its textual richness opens abyss beneath abyss, beneath each deep a deeper deep, as the reader interrogates its elements and lets each question generate an answer that is another question in its turn. (LM, p. 422)

Miller's book is based on the idea that "such a search for grounding or such a testing of the ground is a fundamental feature of literature, as of human existence" (LM p. xvii). While this means that literature is always ethical, philosophical, or religious, it does not mean that the quest for the ground has to be successful – particularly, if one grants, as Miller does, the possibility that these metaphysical components might be resident in language itself rather than in any explicit statements.

The Ethics of Reading (1986), Miller's most recent book, is another fascinating attempt to locate the ground of a major metaphysical concept of Western thought, that of "ethicity". In this function, the book performs a sophisticated investigation of the elusive interface between language and non-linguistic factors. But the *Ethics* also does well as a shrewd vindication of the deconstructionist cause, as a *defensio* against charges of an alleged "nihilism" or ahistoricism in deconstruction. Working along similar lines as its predecessor, the *Ethics* concentrates on passages where an author reads himself. These passages, in which the author becomes the reader and the reader the author, are crucial according to Miller. They yield substantial insights into the "ethics of reading", that "necessary ethical moment in the act of reading as such, a moment neither cognitive, nor political, nor social, nor interpersonal, but properly and independently ethical" (ER, p. 1). Starting out with a powerful deconstruction of a passage from Kant's *Grundlegung zur Metaphysik der Sitten*, Miller proceeds to examples from de Man, George Eliot, Trollope, James, and Benjamin to buttress his claim that any act of reading conditions an inalienable ethical moment. This moment does not emerge, Miller postulates, when language "talks about" ethics, but is rather an inherent feature of language:

> By "the ethics of reading" . . . I mean that aspect of the act of reading in which there is a response to the text that is both necessitated, in the sense that it is a response to an

irresistible demand, and free, in the sense that I must take
responsibility for my response and for the further effects,
"interpersonal", institutional, social, political, or historical,
of my act of reading, for example as that act takes the form
of teaching or of published commentary on a given text.
(ER, p. 43)

As Miller demonstrates in his keen reading of the *Grundlegung*, it is impossible for Kant to derive from the purely
theoretical discourse an unequivocal definition of what
"ethical" means. He shows how the logic of the passage
collapses at the crucial point and how Kant is – because of
his own reasoning – trapped like a sailor between Scylla
and Charybdis. To act truly morally means, if one sticks
to the letter, to act purely from one's own will, without
consideration of the expected result – to act amorally, or
immorally, in other words. At the same time the law,
because it must not in any way be specific, is spelled out
in the *Grundlegung* in a manner so purified of any content
that it becomes perfectly useless as a standard of action.
Miller shows how Kant is only able to make his point by
having recourse to a brief (but famous) narrative digression:
to act ethically, one should never act in any other way, than
so that one's personal maxim could be made a universal
law acceptable for all mankind. Narrative must be used
wherever the purely conceptual discourse produces nothing
but blanks. Ethics "involves narrative as its subversive
accomplice. Storytelling is the impurity which is necessary
in any discourse about the moral law as such, in spite of
the law's austere indifference to persons, stories, and history" (ER, p. 23). But narrative acts as an indefinite postponement of the law and the (good) reader in the end faces
the unreadability of the text rather than a clear example
that would unequivocally illustrate the moral law.

However, in spite of such clear-cut claims as the one
that "ethical judgment and command is a necessary feature

of human language" (ER, p. 46) *The Ethics of Reading*, not atypically, ends in an aporia. Miller is unable to determine whether his experiences are the result of a linguistic or an ontological necessity. Even though he is continuously experiencing the law of the ethics of reading, and is subject to it whenever he is reading, he is unable to confront or access it directly. The law, as Miller quotes Derrida, gives itself without giving itself, and he concedes that it might be that the "necessity of deferring is itself the law to which I am subject" (ER, p. 127). Still, the consequences of his locating "ethicity" in language itself reach beyond this critical impasse. For one thing, the *Ethics of Reading* seriously questions the tacit assumption that language could refer to "ethicity" if it were only used in a refined enough manner. And for another, Miller's book addresses a much greater issue, namely that of the "value" of literature. Forcefully asserting how literature acts as "in some way a cause and not merely an effect", Miller "prevents it from being the relatively trivial study of one of the epiphenomena of society, part of the technological assimilation or assertion of mastery over all features of human life which is called 'the human sciences'" (ER, p. 5).

What is truly fascinating about Miller's criticism are his readings. In spite of a number of seminal theoretical statements, Miller is most of all a brilliant reader. At heart, he prefers reading over theorizing: "A theory is all too easy to refute or deny, but a reading can be controverted only by going through the difficult task of rereading the work in question and proposing an alternative reading" (FR, p. 21). Much of the attractiveness of his interpretations lies in an exceptionally articulate style that mirrors the limpidity of his thinking. Paragraphs, articles, or entire books are well structured, and difficult concepts are analysed with great care and subtlety. (A case in point is "Ariachne's Broken Woof".) The two main characteristics of Miller's critical attitude, rigorousness and creativity, coexist in a singular, distinguished balance. Withal, his rigor does not partake of the linguistic tedium of structuralist analysis nor does his creativity indulge in the much-feared anarchic free-play that would grant an equal validity to any and all interpretations.

Very much like Paul de Man, Miller is particularly interested in those crossovers where language "pulls the rug from under its own feet", i.e. where the text transgresses or contradicts those laws it has, to all outward appearances, created for itself. Rather than dwelling with the problematic conditions of conceptual thought themselves, he uses them as a *point de repère* to close in on the moments of self-contradictoriness inherent in the rhetoric of a given text. In order for him to arrive at such a point, he must follow through an interpretation patiently, with perfectly undivided attention, as far as it will carry him. Once arrived there, he "listens" to the text for answers. Frequently, the passages he examines answer questions that have never been asked. And they fail to answer those questions they are supposed to answer. It is Miller's remarkable ability to perceive these unsolicited answers and to show how they are effects of the ruses of language. Reading is for Hillis Miller – as for Paul de Man – always *mis*reading. An interpretation can neither grasp an originary meaning nor can it encompass all potential readings. This does not simply mean that the number of possible readings is infinite. It means rather that a reading might have to coexist with one or several different or even conflicting readings.

Miller's critical development is a continuum rather than a series of abrupt reversals, as has often been claimed. What he has learned from the New Critics, in other words, and from Georges Poulet, has left its permanent marks. Of course, Miller now sees his readings under different "methodological presuppositions" and he expresses his worries to that effect in the later prefaces to *The Form of Victorian Fiction* or *The Disappearance of God*. Nevertheless, it seems to me that the intelligent readings of his "phenomenological phase" lose very little of their plausibility and convincing stringency, even though such formerly pivotal concepts as the "self" of the author, "Zeitgeist", or "consciousness", have in the meantime become either anathema or at least very problematical. Staying aloof from staunch post-structuralist epistemology, he has blended into his very distinct, pragmatic deconstruction numerous "traditional" elements. Hence his criticism is in essence an exceptionally refined kind of *explication de texte*. This is not to say that Miller's criticism is one step removed from that of his models Jacques Derrida or Paul de Man. Rather it characterizes him as a genuine philologist in the Nietzschean sense, as "ein Lehrer des langsamen Lesens" ("a teacher of slow reading") who professes, above all, remarkably careful, responsible, and acute reading.[5]

Martin Heusser

Miller's present essay, a reading of Hawthorne's "The Minister's Black Veil", is announced in the closing paragraph of *The Ethics of Reading*, where Miller "remain[s] forced to postpone once more the direct confrontation of the law of the ethics of reading, unless that necessity of deferring is itself the law to which I am subject" (ER, p. 127). With this observation he prepares the ground, so to speak, for a demonstration that it is reading, not history, or tradition, or ethics, from which we deduce ethical forms of behavior. "In order to test that possibility", Miller proposes, "it will be necessary to read novels and tales by Eliot, Trollope, James, and others, perhaps Kleist, Hawthorne" (ER, p. 127). Miller's essay on Hawthorne's story is part of that test. It analyses the various ways in which we attempt, as readers of fiction or as citizens of Milford, to look behind appearance. After one of his slowest and most admirably meticulous readings, we learn – we *learn* it because we resist it – that the story of which the minister's black veil is an allegory "does not respond to any of our attempts to read it" (p. 97). This, surely, is a curious thing for Miller to claim after this reader has just read "The Minister's Black Veil", as well as Miller's essay about that story. I must, therefore, ask what Miller means by reading. I shall attempt this, first, by way of a crucial passage in Nietzsche's *Birth of Tragedy*, a passage that prefaces or charts Miller's own deconstructive reading. I shall then try to apply the ensuing theory to a passage in *The Ethics of Reading*, where Miller translates Kant. Both as theme and as a translation, that passage will exemplify the untranslatability of an original, or the unreadability of an original meaning.

The conclusions, finally, both of my argument and of Miller's essay, may be anticipated: "Aporia, impasse, *malconfort*, in which one can neither sit nor stand" (DD, p. 30). The implications of Miller's particular "*malconfort*", however, seem to me to point more in the direction of Kierkegaard's paradox as vestibule to a spiritual world than to Nietzsche's joyous affirmation of a world with neither falsity nor truth. Despite his gestures of spiritual modesty and confessions of his failure to read, Miller seems to discover something that cannot be thought. Since it cannot be thought, it is a discovery whose fate it is to be tragically misread at every attempt by virtue of a linguistic necessity, which requires for its functionality its own ontologic self-deception. Whether that can be summed up as "the negations of deconstruction [which] represent something like the thematic side of the tragic, or perhaps only the pathetic",[6] is perhaps beside the point, since deconstruction is not, as we shall see, simply a negation.

Assuming that mathematicians, too, are privy to the "abysmal discomfort" of the deconstructionist at "the moment when logic fails" (SR, p. 338), Miller's interest in mathematics, professed on the occasion of his visit to Bucknell, might have yielded, had he so decided, not so different a career. In his essay "Ariadne's Thread: Repetition and the Narrative Line", Miller quotes Pater's story of the "strenuous, self-possessed, much honored monastic student" whose twelfth volume of a mathematical treatise suddenly submits to "a violent beam, a blaze, a new light, revealing . . . a hundred truths unguessed at before, yet a curse, as it turned out, to its receiver, in dividing hopelessly against itself the well-ordered kingdom of his thought" (AT, pp. 59–60). Reading his essay "Stevens' Rock and Criticism as Cure, II" with its Socratic notion of a "clear distinction" between "Socratic, theoretical" and "tragic, or uncanny critics" (SR, p. 335), one realizes that Miller subscribes to "*Wissenschaftlichkeit*" only to carry it "far enough" (SR, p. 338), to a point where method becomes metaphor, where reading yields momentarily a vision of philosophical truth – or, alas, only "an image, a figure, or a myth" (SR, p. 338). Such, for example, is the discovery of Miller's reading of himself in his 1975 Preface to *The Disappearance of God*, where God's very disappearance appears *sous rature*: "it appears that the relation between my present work and that of over a decade ago is more than simply negative. It may be in the nature of literature that investigations of it initiated according to a given hypothesis will lead, if carried far enough, to insights which call that hypothesis into question" (pp. xii–xiii).

The passage from Nietzsche's *Birth of Tragedy* quoted in his essay "Stevens' Rock and Criticism as Cure, II" seems exemplary of Miller's interrogative strategies. The passage, one might imagine, bears some biographical references, not only to the implications of Miller's mathematical road not taken, but also to his turn from the well-ordered world of New Critical formalism to deconstruction:

Denn die Peripherie des Kreises der Wissenschaft hat unendlich viele Punkte, und während noch gar nicht abzusehen ist, wie jemals der Kreis völlig ausgemessen werden könnte, so trifft doch der edle und begabte Mensch, noch vor der Mitte seines

Daseins und unvermeidlich, auf solche Grenzpunkte der Peripherie, wo er in das Unaufhellbare starrt. Wenn er hier zu seinem Schrecken sieht, wie die Logik sich an diesen Grenzen um sich selbst ringelt und endlich sich in den Schwanz beisst – da bricht die neue Form der Erkenntnis durch, die tragische Erkenntnis, *die, um nur ertragen zu werden, als Schutz und Heilmittel die Kunst braucht.*[7]

I had come across Nietzsche's remarkable passage through Francis Golffing's translation of Nietzsche's *Geburt der Tragödie*:

The periphery of science has an infinite number of points. Every noble and gifted man has, before reaching the midpoint of his career, come up against some point of the periphery that defied his understanding, quite apart from the fact that we have no way of knowing how the area of the circle is ever fully charted. When the inquirer, having pushed to the circumference, realizes how logic in that place curls about itself and bites its own tail, he is struck with a new kind of perception: a tragic perception, which requires, to make it tolerable, the remedy of art.[8]

But "the remedy of art" is a deception, an illusion around and about which Nietzsche's text circles and curls from its beginning through various repetitions – new beginnings, summaries, and temporary conclusions – to its end, not its conclusion. The remedy, we have read and reread and read again one page from the end, is the veil of Apollo, "those countless illusions of fair semblance which any moment make life worth living and whet our appetite for the next moment" (BT, p. 145). Of that repeated moment in Nietzsche's book, when the veil of Apollo spreads over the tragic perception, we need the right translation to examine precisely the quality and constitution of the veil. In his essay "Stevens' Rock . . . ", Miller uses Walter Kaufmann's translation where Nietzsche's "*als Schutz und Heilmittel die*

Kunst" is rendered as "art as a protection and remedy" (SR, p. 346).⁹ The difference between Kaufmann's and Golffing's translations is decisive. Golffing's "remedy of art" is a metaphor substituted for Nietzsche's simile "*als Schutz und Heilmittel die Kunst*", i.e. art as remedy. It is in that subtle difference that Nietzsche's tragic stance appears. The simile negates the metaphor: art is not identifiable with remedy but only identifiable in its likeness to – but then also in its unlikeness to – remedy. Nietzsche's "*tragische Erkenntnis*", then, is a perception that is tragic precisely because, while being tempted by the possibility of the metaphoric equation of art and remedy, the tragic realization calls attention to that equation as a deception; as Kaufmann translates, art is "as a remedy", which is to say, not in essence a remedy itself. The simile persuades as, momentarily, we believe that art is remedy. But the simile as a simile, just as art as remedy, betrays the hope in remedy, it invokes but simultaneously revokes the equation. The metaphor is silent about such a deception, it deceives better, it forgets its epistemology, it does not hold us up, it is the ontologic misreading of a linguistic indeterminacy. Since it is indeterminate, "art as remedy", with its vacillating keeping and breaking of its promise, requires slow reading. In Nietzsche's "art as remedy", logic bites its own tail and art is not so different from the circumference of science. Art, Hillis Miller might say, is a portmanteau word, a word for something that is both similarity and disimilarity (AT, p. 66). In his review of Joseph Riddel's *The Inverted Bell*, Miller uses a footnote by Derrida to draw attention to the problem of translation as exemplary for "the problem of the possible sameness of the different". He adds further that "[t]he question of the relation of sameness and difference is a traditional metaphysical problem, perhaps even *the* metaphysical problem" (DD, p. 26). Nietzsche's Dionysos-Apollo dialectic is yet another instance of this problem of translation, just as this is the case with the minister's black veil, which, veiling something unknowable, is translated into "The Minister's Black Veil", which, in turn, "demands to be 'read' in the sense of glossed, or translated, in a potentially interminable commentary" (p. 26).

Art consoles but it only consoles as art: not "art is remedy" but "art as remedy". The copula "is", Derrida points out, paraphrasing Nietzsche, "transform[s] a 'subjective excitation' into an objective judgement, into a pretension to truth".[10] "Art *is* remedy" is an empty promise, a false, perhaps a temptingly false claim to a truth that cannot be translated or read.

Nietzsche's dialectic "between the insatiable thirst for knowledge and man's tragic dependency on art" (BT, p. 96) unravels the pretension to truth. But the unravelling in Nietzsche's book is in itself nothing more than a subjective excitement about Wagner's music which allows for no more than "a brief moment" of insight into "the struggle, the pain, the destruction of appearances" (BT, p. 102). Wagner's music stands, for Nietzsche, as the unmediated voice of nature, otherwise there is "only appearance, from which no bridge leads to the true reality, the heart of the world" (GT, p. 119, my trans.). Thus any attempt to bridge, to traverse, or to translate this voice of nature, or this heart of the world, inevitably carries across as well its own destruction. The word *metaphor* from Greek *metaphora*, to transfer, to carry across, does not keep its promise. "Language promises, but what it promises is itself", as Hillis Miller writes in *The Ethics of Reading* (p. 35). The gap between essence and appearance cannot be traversed, while Golffing's metaphor steps over it as if nothing were there. But indeed nothing is there, for Nietzsche's "art as remedy" promises insight into a truth that would be invisible without the illusory mediation of art. But since that mediation is illusory, can we ever say, then, we have "seen" the truth? Has Job "seen" the truth after the "folly" of his words? "Art as a remedy" is a catachresis, "the violent, forced, or abusive use of a term from another realm to name something which has no 'proper' name" (AT, p. 72). For just what is it that art remedies? We do not know. Merely to "feel it" in one's hour of death, as Arnold's Empedocles does, only leads Arnold back to the Classical world of appearances. Empedocles, "the singer who goes out into the empty space between man, nature, and the gods, opening again a channel for their intercommunication" (LM, p. 23) cannot trust his song. His song is ambiguous and paradoxical as is the illusion of art. If Empedocles' space is empty, his leap into the crater is a catachresis. It is the remedy not for an existential *Abgrund* but an epistemological *Ungrund*. But if his space is not empty, if "a channel for . . . intercommunication" is left open, art is the remedy for an existential *Abgrund* rather than an *Ungrund*, perhaps the remedy for a mystical "force", or "matter", a psychological remedy for "an irresistible demand", an "I must", or as Walter Benjamin's phrase suggests, a remedy for "*das in allen Sprachen Gemeinte*" (cf. ER, p. 123). However, "[a]ll these phrases and names are", as Miller points out repeatedly, "violent, forced, and abusive" because "to name the abyss is to cover it, to make a fiction or icon of it, a likeness that is no likeness" (LM, p. 419). Indeed, all these phrases have in common with Miller's Empedocles that they wander in an empty space between the gods, men, and nature. They oscillate between various philosophical positions without finding certainty in any one of them. Hence, as Miller writes in "Stevens' Rock and Criticism as Cure", "[t]he paradox of the *mise en abyme* is the following: without the production of some schema, some 'icon', there can be no glimpse of the abyss, no vertigo of the underlying nothingness. Any such schema, however, both opens the chasm, creates it or reveals it, and at the same time fills it up, covers it over by naming it, gives the groundless a ground, the bottomless a bottom" (SR, p. 12). Empedocles, the singer who goes out into the empty space, is such an icon.

Golffing's "ontologic" translation denies this perception

of the duplicity of the ground. It may be coincidental but
consistent with this denial that Golffing also forgets and
leaves untranslated the "*Schrecken*", the horror, the vertigo
which occurs in Arnold's poem, or in Nietzsche's text,
when the tragic realization breaks through. Paul de Man
in his discussion of *The Birth of Tragedy*, mentions various
dramatizations – and Nietzsche's noble and gifted man's
horror may be one – by which "the possibility of this
bridge, of this translation (Nietzsche speaks of 'übersetzen'
and 'überbrücken') [is] performed in the metaphorical narrative by means of which Dionysos can enter into a world
of appearances and still somehow remain Dionysos".[11] But
de Man's "somehow" indicates that Dionysos must
compromise his identity just as Apollo must compromise
his insight. Dionysos here performs the same dubious legislation as does the Law in *The Ethics of Reading*. Like
Nietzsche's logic, Kant's law curls about itself. In "Ariadne's Thread" Miller lays the etymological ground for the
similarity. Like logic "*lex* is from lege-, to collect. It is the
same root as that for 'logic' and 'coil'" (AT, p. 69).

Miller's reading of Kant is itself implicated, folded into,
this bifurcating, ambiguous, etymology. Carried far enough
it becomes "the story of error"[12] in the same way in which
Ruskin's etymology of the word *labyrinth* performs a "false,
but suggestively false" reading, epitomizing that all readings are "far from providing a benign escape from the
maze" (SR, p. 337). In his discussion of a passage in
Kant's *Grundlegung zur Metaphysik der Sitten*, Miller draws
attention to an "entanglement of narration and ethics" (ER,
p. 25). This entanglement, Miller observes, "is obliquely
revealed in Kant's insertion, just at this place in his argument, of his celebrated formulation that I should act, if I
wish to act ethically, at all times and places as if the private
maxim according to which I choose to do or not to do were
to be made the universal law for all mankind" (ER, p. 25).
These and other remarks preface the Kantian passage with

its revealing "place", all of which Miller cautiously prefaces as "Kant's words, or rather the words of his translator, with some of Kant's own words inserted parenthetically" (ER, p. 26).

In spite of such cautious qualification, I would like to draw attention, in what follows, to a narrative entanglement in Miller's own reading of Kant and the oblique revelation of that entanglement in a certain "place". I presume that such a demonstration will prove the validity of Miller's central observations about Kant's argument and that those observations will also apply to Miller's argument: "Narrative as a fundamental activity of the human mind, the power to make fictions, to tell stories to oneself or to others, serves for Kant as the absolutely necessary bridge without which there would be no connection between the law as such and any particular ethical rule of behavior" (ER, p. 28). Miller's project is similar to Kant's and similarly doomed to reveal (obliquely) fundamental activities of the human mind and necessary bridges. Kant wants to lay the foundation for the metaphysics of morals; Miller wants to lay the foundations for the metaphysics of reading. If narrative is "fundamental" and "absolutely necessary" for Kant, it will also be so for Miller; and if narrative entanglements happen to Kant, we may presume, they may happen to anyone. As I have indicated, Miller identifies Kant's narrative entanglement in a particular "place" in Kant's argument (ER, p. 25). I will in turn identify such a place in Miller's argument.

The place where this occurs is ironic. It is exactly the same place for Miller as it is for Kant, which implies that Kant's narrative entanglements, perhaps any narrative entanglement, can only be paraphrased, or "explained", through further entanglements. The entanglement occurs in that oblique modal conjunction "als so" which Miller translates as "as if". I should act, Miller had paraphrased on the previous page, if I wish to act ethically, "as if" the private maxim were the universal law. "I must act", he repeats, "as if (als so) that were the case" (ER, p. 26). The modal conjunction "as if" throws a bridge across the gap between the private maxim and the universal law: "als so" imples "a whole fictive narrative" (ER, p. 26). "*Als so*" is rendered by the translator in Miller's book, literally, as "in such a way": "I should never act in such a way that I could not also will that my maxim should be a universal law [d.i. ich soll niemals anders verfahren, als so, *dass ich auch wollen könne, meine Maxim solle ein allgemeines Gesetz werden*"] (ER, p. 26). Miller's "as if" with its ensuing narrative theory is a curious addendum. It is his own fundamental activity, his power to make fictions, his story added to "Kant's words" and "the words of his translator".

If indeed the story of Miller's "as if" reveals a fundamental and absolute necessity, it may be one inevitable narrative part of what (in his chapter on Paul de Man) he calls an "intricate sequence" of references to the extra-linguistic. But like that elusive thing called "reality" which will not validate language (ER, p. 44), the German text will not validate the translation, so that Miller's translation is "the revelation of its aberrancy" and "the expression in a veiled form of the impossibility of reading that revelation of aberrancy, (ER, p. 45).[13] Behind this veiled form, if we could retrace chronologically an intricate sequence of mis-translations, we might glimpse the linguistic inheritance of what Miller calls in *The Linguistic Moment* "that primal misnaming" (LM, p. 420). That is to say, Miller's own "narrative" seems based on the assumption of what Walter Benjamin calls "a lost original" (ER, p. 125), or a "law as such", which cannot be translated into a particular language or into particular ethical rules of behavior other than by metaphors which carry across their own destruction. Miller's literary rather than literal translation, then, is an example of a linguistic predicament elucidated by his remarks (quoted above) about the problem of translation. For a similar problem Kant posits in his *Critique of Judgement* a "symbolic hypotyposis" which is "a concept which only reason can think and to which no sensible intuition can be adequate" (§ 59). This concept differs from the so-called "schematic hypotyposis", which is based on empirical data and "demonstrative". But "[o]ur language is replete", Kant adds, "with . . . indirect representations, based on analogy, where the expression does not contain the actual schema for the concept, but contains merely a symbol for our reflection" (§ 59; my trans.).[14]

Miller's reading and translation of Kant's passage in *The Ethics of Reading* is a reading of the text as symbolic rather than as schematic. This seems to me to be justified even though Kant's maxim never to act "in such a way" reads as a schematic, demonstrative expression, referring to an empirical example. But the example of a moral maxim that is also a universal law cannot be made. Or, to put this differently, Kant's implicit promise in his demonstrative "such" a particular "way", will be taken back not only by the epistemological impossibility to will and to enact and to verify a general by a particular law but also by the subjunctives "könne" and "solle". The mode of these verbs underscores both the epistemological impossibility of Kant's maxim and the absurdly paradoxical way in which practice must follow by preceding that upon which it is founded. If Kant's subjunctives "könne" and "solle" indicate the imaginative, or "symbolic" nature of his argument, Miller's translation of "als so" into "as if" can be said to follow these literary resonances (or intuitions, as Kant might put it) of Kant's rhetoric. Like Hawthorne's, Kant's genre, finally, is a parable telling the story of a universal law in "opaque symbols that resist translation into perspicuous concepts" (p. 78).

There is more than a hint of the impossibility of a literal translation of the original law in Kant's own first part of the *Grundlegung*, when he admits that his respect for the *allgemeine Gesetzgebung* (the law as such) cannot be grounded: *"für diese [die allgemeine Gesetzgebung] aber zwingt mir die Vernunft unmittelbare Achtung ab, von der ich zwar jetzt noch nicht einsehe, worauf sie sich gründe (welches der Philosoph untersuchen mag).* [Towards that, however, reason forces me to respond with immediate respect, although I do not at this point understand on what that reason is founded (which may be examined by the philosopher]".[15] To be sure, Miller is not the philosopher of Kant's dismissive parenthesis. Kant's parenthesis, suggesting that the philosopher may inquire into the question of the ground for his reason or respect, is passed on by Miller to "others" who in their turn are to perform a "full reading of Kant's third *Kritik*" to test "the solidity of this ground" (SG, p. 30). But it is implicit in Miller's, and I assume as well in Kant's, delegation of this task to philosophers that the solidity of this ground cannot be established. Miller's predicament is thus consonant with, and called for, by Kant's own problem in the *Grundlegung*. Both the origin of Kant's thinking, which is his desire for a laying of the ground for the law, and Miller's original (text), which is Kant's *Grundlegung zur Metaphysik der Sitten*, cannot be translated, strictly speaking, but require – I repeat the quotation from above – "the metaphorical narrative by means of which Dionysos can enter into a world of appearance and still somehow remain Dionysos". De Man's "somehow" is charmingly indicative of the imprecision, the self-destructive fictionality of both Kant's and Miller's arguments. Kant's dismissive parenthesis suggesting that philosophers might occupy themselves with the problem of the *Grundlegung* alludes self-consciously to his own discourse as not philosophical – and so does Miller's half-ironic reference to the "others" who may vainly test the solidity of Kant's ground. The passage from literature to philosophy, or from rhetoric to knowledge, is interminable.[16]

Miller's philosophic position, which is in part grounded on Nietzsche's, a work without a ground, is thus, like Nietzsche's work, post-philosophic. His theory of narrative as a fundamental activity of the human mind to bridge the abyss between appearance and truth is all inclusive, including the philosopher as a teller of tales. Thus what is to be shown in the "never innocent" (ER, p. 11) inclusion of Kant in *The Ethics of Reading* is that in "that blank space where the presumed purely conceptual language of philosophy fails or is missing" (ER, p. 24), the sheer rhetorical force of a fictional argument allows the construction of a flying bridge and a hasty crossing before the abyss swallows that bridge as well.

Miller admits to performing such a hasty crossing in his use of the theory of prosopopoeia as a "tool" to read "The Minister's Black Veil". To confess his failure to read, through his inevitable use of a theoretical tool, however, is tantamount to Kant's self-conscious use of "als so". If that is for Kant the "solution to an apparently insoluble knot in thinking . . . where the necessity of narrative enters" (ER, p. 28), the same would be true for Miller's use of a "tool" whose validity he ultimately calls into question. Like Kant, whom he imagines as muttering to himself, "we must . . . perform a little experiment, enter in imagination into a little fiction, an 'as if' or 'als so'" (ER, p. 28), Miller proposes the same fiction through his admitted projections of human faces behind the veil of the text. And "though it endures being translated into the unverifiable concepts which eat it up", Hawthorne's story, according to Miller, makes similar gestures as does Kant's transcendent law in respect to the interpretive hunger of its readers. Miller quotes Bartleby's "I should prefer not to" from Melville's story, as a response to these interpretive demands, adding, "like Bartleby's phrase, with its conditional 'should', its gently indecisive 'prefer', both inhibiting the 'not' from being the negative of some positive and thereby something we can make part of some dialectical reasoning. 'The Minister's Black Veil' is neither positive nor negative". The minister himself becomes a spokesman for these epistemological problems, responding "in terms of 'if' and 'perhaps'", as Miller points out, to his fiancée's hermeneutical curiosity.

   The untranslatability of a literal or original truth ties the insoluble knot in Kant's thinking, the impasse where "as if" is proposed, and where the grammatical mode becomes the subjunctive: "könne" and "solle", not the philosophical indicative, "kann" and "soll". Miller's readings thrive on this subjunctive potential, which is, of course, nothing else than what Aristotle called poetry: "a kind of thing that might happen, i.e. what is possible". Miller's translation of Kant's "als so" thus conveys a *literary*, an unphilosophical knowledge contaminated by Kant's own literary knowledge. Both texts, Miller's and Kant's, are versions of the same story and both have a similar epistemological relationship with their original, namely that the gap between a text and its *Grund* is always absolute but by the same token, always open: "I am only able to tell stories about it", or, "I am unable, finally, to know whether in this experience I am subject to a linguistic necessity or to an ontological one" (ER, p. 127).

Finally, however, "the temptation to ontologize is almost irresistible" (ER, p. 122). Similarly, we have noted how easy it is to misread Nietzsche's "art as a remedy" as "the remedy of art". By what law are we forced to such misreading or mistranslation? Is Golffing's mistake inevitable? If so, then the reader transgresses his ethical obligation towards the text or towards art; he does not read, he misreads. "What is only a linguistic necessity or imperative", Miller concludes, "is infallibly misread as a transcendental one" (ER, p. 122). Art, finally and infallibly, *is* remedy, the necessary pretension to truth. By the same necessity Nietzsche himself on the same page speaks metaphorically of the "*Netz der Kunst*", the "net of art". It is this pretension to truth which Arnold might have had in mind when in his essay "The Study of Poetry" he predicted that "[m]ore and more mankind will discover that we have to turn to poetry to interpret life to us, to console us, to sustain us. . . . What now passes . . . for religion and philosophy will be replaced by poetry".[17] This amounts to the same as when Miller admits, "I am unable to avoid making the linguistic mistake of responding to a necessity of language as if it had ontological force and authority" (ER, p. 127).

In the face of this argument one is tempted to entertain the possibility that Miller has been lured into a dialectical argument between language on the one side and what he can say about it on the other side. For how, within a linguistic system, are we to determine we are "making the linguistic mistake"? Is Miller, in claiming such a mistake, taking back his professed inability to know whether in his literary experience he is subject to a linguistic or to an ontological experience? Like M. H. Abrams, who observes in his essay "The Deconstructive Angel" that Miller "does not entirely and consistently commit himself to the consequences of his premises",[18] one might suspect that here Miller comments on his experience from outside of his linguistic predicament. But in entertaining this suspicion we ourselves tacitly assume an epistemological ground and resting place exterior to the language we use. However, we are not exempt from Miller's linguistic mistake.

Within ten or so lines before its closure, *The Ethics of Reading* itself performs the tragic gesture of art, arriving at yet another one of the points on the periphery of this book's inquiry. To read Miller closely and slowly, we must, at this point, give up any extra-linguistic position or identity, which allows for a dialectic argument between ontology and language, and move with Miller within the Nietzschean circle: here, as I have predicted, is "aporia, impasse, *malconfort*, in which one can neither sit nor stand". If language by necessity pretends to have ontological force and authority ("as if it had") and if this pretense is recognized as such, then this force and authority cease to exist, giving permission only to "art as a remedy". The linguistic mistake, however, is to forget that the vehicle of our "recognition" is itself unreliable. The linguistic mistake is a mistake insofar as we always inevitably participate in that unreliability. But how can we know *that* as true? – By making the linguistic mistake of responding to a necessity of language as if it had ontological force and authority.

To understand the unreliability of language we might best turn to the allegorical example of the veil of Apollo, or the minister's veil. In these examples the unreliability resides in the indeterminable question of whether the meaning of these coverings lies solely in their material reality or in what that material reality conceals. This problem has a mythological precursor in Moses' veiling after his ascent onto Mount Sinai in the book of Exodus – a myth which lends the weight and justification of the archetype to the telling of Hawthorne's story and to Miller's hermeneutical curiosity. Moses' epistemological position in relation to the Law he is to bring down from the mountain is elaborately expressed in that biblical narrative. One such expression may be in Moses' permission to see only God's "back parts" (Ex. 33:23) – I say permission, but it is also, of course, a partial prohibition against seeing God face to face (cf. Ex. 33:20). In spite of, or is it because of, these expressions of his mediated access to God, Moses' face shines and he covers it with a veil when he descends from the mountain (Ex. 34:29,33) so that, like the minister's veil in Miller's commentary, that story too becomes "a veil we would pierce or lift" (p. 77). Much of Moses' divine authority, which turns into the political and ethical laws of his people, originates from two possibilities: "because he had been speaking with the Lord" (Ex. 34:29) or because he had put a veil over his face. The fact that tradition has handed down this story to us as religion seems to prove Miller's observation that to ontologize is almost irresistible. We cannot read the veil itself, but only what it signifies. But to verify our ontologic reading is impossible. Our linguistic instrument is too persuasive to read the indeterminacy itself; we read, irresistibly, too much.

So persuasive, indeed, is the interpreter's tool, so tight the protection and remedy of his skill, that it is impossible to know whether art protects us either from the terrible truth or from the terror of its absence. Neither can we say whether the terror we experience in either case might be authentic or a traditional dramatization of this very predicament, or whether we fancy only that we need the consolation and protection of art. In these latter proposals, both Arnold and Nietzsche not only resemble each other but also reveal, through their vocabulary, the echoes of a Platonic or Christian metaphysics. But there is no ground for such a vocabulary, except for the bricolage of a tradition, just as there may be no reason for consolation. From the perspective of a deconstructive reading, neither is there any reason to distinguish between the existential *Abgrund* and the nihilistic *Ungrund*; our misreadings cover, cure, redeem one and all.

By this linguistic necessity, of nevertheless grounding, focusing, or reasoning, a deconstructionist reading will not be spared the necessity of lifting its own veil and the laying bare of its own inherited or fabricated metaphysics. A place has by necessity to be reached where one can sit or stand and which orders and arrests the indefinite potential of the ways Dionysos may want to appear: as absence, presence, good or evil. "As long as we have not identified the law by which a text can be made reasonable, explicable, it is as if we have come face to face with an immeasurable existence aloof from us, perhaps malign, perhaps benign, in any case something we have not yet mastered and assimilated into what we already know" (SG, p. 20). What knowledge thus accomplishes is effectively to diminish the potential of truth to representational or manageable size by which it may be tragically misread. It is that harbored potential, allegorically offered and epistemologically refused, which might define the literary text as literary, and it is this which might account for Miller's canonical choices for his readings. Perhaps only literary texts hold ontological promises.

Since these promises are never kept, or since it can never be verified what is behind the veil, the reader's infallible ontologizing becomes itself an allegory of the literary potential. By taking what is not freely given, Miller is forced to claim an insight that should be denied by his best intention to read slowly and only what is there. Miller quotes Hans-Jost Frey to this effect in an epigraph to chapter 3 of *The Ethics of Reading*, and again in the text itself: "Every construction, every system, – that is, every text – has within itself the ignorance of its own exterior as the rupture of its coherence which it cannot account for" (ER, p. 56). Such ruptures occur in Nietzsche's redemptive misreading of art as "a remedy and a protection" or to Arnold in his similar misreading of poetry as "consoling" and "sustaining". Because of Empedocles's refusal to adhere to such fictions he remains an enigmatic riddle that must be rejected and disowned. The same exteriority ruptures Miller's argument in the present essay: "Have I not, not through some remediable inadvertence or forgetting, but through an ineluctable compulsion, unavoidably used as the 'tool' of reading the very thing I have most wanted to put in question . . .?". Once it is made conscious, as it is in Miller's text, this rupturing exterior threatens to invalidate the insight it has allowed. Neither can this be avoided through Miller's proposal to read "what the texts actually say" (SG, p. 28). The proposed "actuality" is itself an ontologic temptation, positing a literality which suggests that language obeys a guiding thread, or has a governing critical principle, rather than being subjected to its own indeterminacy. At "the most uncanny moment" therefore even the most "untheoretical" reading turns "all too shrewdly rational" (SR, p. 343). The *mise en abyme* par excellence occurs when the uncanny critic must compromise his insight by an "ordering of the abyss" (SR, pp. 347–48), which resembles all too much the Socratic critic's "rational ordering of literary study" (SR, p. 335).

Nevertheless, there are no short-cuts to this reversal of

positions. When in the closing pages of this essay, Miller "doubt[s] the validity of [his] personifying projections" or the identity of the author-persona, his doubt draws a wider diameter of Nietzsche's periphery of science. While it is again proven here that, as Nietzsche says, "we have no way of knowing how the area of the circle is ever fully charted", the wider drawing of the circle of science can only be done by those, like Miller, who "push to the circumference". For this achievement Miller's essay on "The Minister's Black Veil" deserves our admiration.

In the face of the arduous way Nietzsche charts the circumference of knowledge, we should admit the foolhardiness, perhaps the impossibility of prefacing Miller's work. Like Dante who famously begins his *Commedia, "nel mezzo del camin di nostra vita"*, Nietzsche grants insight to the noble and gifted man only at some advanced stage, I suspect, not too many years "before midway in his career". Neither does Pater's strenuous, much-honored monastic student reach his blinding insight in the second volume of his treatise but in the twelfth. Finally, with Miller's work, of which the present piece is a generous and brilliant example, we shall not find ourselves at the circumference before we have read it.

Harold Schweizer

NOTES

1   "Philologie nämlich ist jene ehrwürdige Kunst, welche von ihrem Verehrer vor allem eins heischt, beiseite gehn, sich Zeit lassen, still werden, langsam werden–, als eine Goldschmiedekunst und -kennerschaft des *Wortes*, die lauter feine vorsichtige Arbeit abzutun hat und nichts erreicht, wenn sie es nicht *lento* erreicht . . . sie selbst wird nicht so leicht irgend womit fertig, sie lehrt *gut* lesen, das heisst langsam, tief, rück- und vorsichtig, mit Hintergedanken mit offengelassenen Türen, mit zarten Fingern und Augen lesen . . ." The passage is cited from Nietzsche's preface to *Morgenröte*

(*Daybreak*), in Miller's preface to *The Linguistic Moment*.

2   Poulet taught at the University of Edinburgh between 1927 and 1951, at Johns Hopkins between 1952 and 1957, and from 1958 on at the University of Zurich.

3   Some of the far-reaching implications of the nature of cata-chresis are worked out later in detail in a powerful but difficult and sporadically elusive article on Wallace Stevens' "Red Fern", "Impossible Metaphor: Stevens's 'The Red Fern' as Example", *The Lesson of Paul de Man, Yale French Studies* 69 (1985) pp. 150–62.

4   "On Edge" is reprinted in Morris Eaves and Michael Fischer (eds.), *Romanticism and Contemporary Criticism*, (Ithaca: Cornell University Press, 1986). The quotation appears on p. 101. The collection also contains M. H. Abrams' "Con-struing and Deconstructing", a detailed response to Miller's "On Edge" and a critical evaluation of deconstruction in general.

5   Miller quotes this definition from Nietzsche's preface to *Morgenröte* (*Daybreak*) in the epigraph to his Preface to *The Linguistic Moment* (p. xiii):

> Diese Vorrede kommt spät, aber nicht zu spät, was liegt im Grunde an fünf, sechs Jahren? Ein solches Buch, ein solches Problem hat keine Eile; überdies sind wir beide Freunde des *lento*, ich ebensowohl als mein Buch. Man ist nicht umsonst Philologe gewesen, man ist es vielleicht noch, das will sagen, ein Lehrer des langsamen Lesens: – endlich schreibt man auch langsam. (Schlechta, 1016)

> This preface, however, does not arrive late, how much difference could five or six years make? Such a book, such a problem requires no hurry; moreover, we are both friends of the *lento*, I as much as my book. One has not been a philologist in vain, perhaps one still is, this means, a teacher of slow reading: – after all, one writes slowly, too. (My trans.)

6   Murray Krieger, *Words about Words about Words: Theory, Criticism, and the Literary Text* (Baltimore: The Johns Hop-kins University Press, 1988) p. 57.

7   In   Karl   Schlechta   (ed.),   *Friedrich   Nietzsche: Werke*

(Frankfurt: Ullstein Materialien, 1969; rpt. 1980) pp. 86–87. References to this edition are abbreviated in the text as GT.

8 *The Birth of Tragedy* and *The Genealogy of Morals* (New York: Doubleday, 1956) p. 95. References to this edition are abbreviated in the text as BT.

9 Cf. *The Birth of Tragedy* and *The Case of Wagner* (New York: Vintage Books, 1967) p. 98.

10 "The Supplement of Copula: Philosophy *before* Linguistics" (1976); rpt. In Josué V. Harari (ed.), *Textual Strategies: Perspectives in Post–Structuralist Criticism* (Ithaca: Cornell University Press, 1979) p. 84.

11 *Allegories of Reading* (New Haven: Yale University Press, 1979) p. 101.

12 G. Douglas Atkins, *Reading Deconstruction* (Lexington: The University Press of Kentucky, 1983) pp. 86, 88.

13 After the completion of this essay I received the potentially devastating news that Miller had changed his translation of Kant's phrase for the paperback edition of *The Ethics of Reading*. The change does fulfill better Benjamin's idea of transparency, but it does so without liberating, as Benjamin puts it, the "heavy and foreign sense" behind Kant's language. The pertinent passage from the paperback edition reads as follows: "I must act in such a way (als so) that it is as if I were assuming that to be the case. In that "as if" a whole fictive narrative is implicit" (ER, p. 26). Although this translation has a more literal relationship to Kant's text, the notorious "as if" reappears twice; in the second sentence it remains unchanged compared to the hardback edition; in both the second and first sentences, however, it serves – and I think paradoxically so – as an attempted explanation of what "precisely" might be meant by "in such a way". This illustrates my observations about Kant's own phrasing: Like Kant's "als so", Miller's demonstrative "in such a way" promises the imminent revelation of a truth. But the promise is not kept. As I have noted, Kant's subjunctives "könne" and "solle" withdraw the promise of the revelation, but instead promise more text, both by Kant (his examples of his maxim) as well as by philosophers who might busy themselves with the grounding of the universal law (see p. 24). Trying to disentangle Miller's convoluted "in such a

way that it is as if I were assuming that . . ." with its own promise and layered qualifications we end up, I trust, with an argument which the reader can follow above.

14   Immanuel Kant, *Kritik der Urteilskraft* (Stuttgart: Reclam 1976). Cf. *Critique of Judgement*, trans. Werner S. Pluhar (Indianapolis: Ackett Publishing Company, 1987).

15   Karl Vorländer (ed.), *Grundlegung zur Metaphysik der Sitten* (Hamburg: Felix Meiner Verlag, 1962) p. 22.

16   Cf. Shoshana Felman, "Psychoanalysis and Education: Teaching Terminable and Interminable", in Con Davis and Schleifer (eds.), *Contemporary Literary Criticism* (New York: Longman, 1989) pp. 608–9).

17   In A. Dwight Culler (ed.), *Poetry* and *Criticism of Matthew Arnold* (Boston: Houghton Mifflin, 1961) p. 306. Cf. also SG, pp. 25ff.

18   *Critical Inquiry* 3, no. 3 (Spring 1977) 437

REFERENCES

The following works by J. Hillis Miller are cited in the Introduction:

Charles Dickens: The World of His Novels (Cambridge: Harvard University Press, 1958) (CD)

The Disappearance of God: Five Nineteenth-Century Writers (Cambridge: Harvard University Press, 1963; repr. New York: Schocken Books, 1965) (DG).

"The Literary Criticism of Georges Poulet", *Modern Language Notes* 78, no. 5 (December 1963).

Poets of Reality: Six Twentieth-Century Writers (Cambridge: Harvard University Press, 1965; repr. New York: Atheneum, 1969) (PR).

"The Geneva School: The Criticism of Marcel Raymond, Albert Béguin, Georges Poulet, Jean Rousset, Jean-Pierre Richard, and Jean Starobinski", *The Critical Quarterly* 8, no. 4 (Winter 1966).

The Form of Victorian Fiction (Notre Dame, Ind.: University of Notre Dame Press, 1968; repr. Cleveland: Arete Press, 1979) (FVF)

Thomas Hardy: Distance and Desire (Cambridge: Harvard University Press, 1970) (TH).

"Geneva or Paris? The Recent Work of Georges Poulet", *University of Toronto Quarterly* 39, no. 3 (April 1970) (GP).

"Deconstructing the Deconstructors", *Diacritics* 5, no. 2 (Summer 1975) (DD).

"Stevens' Rock and Criticism as Cure", *The Georgia Review* 30, nos. 1–2 (Spring-Summer 1976) (SR).

"Ariadne's Thread: Repetition and the Narrative Line", *Critical Inquiry* 3, no. 1 (Autumn 1976) (AT).

"Ariachne's Broken Woof", *The Georgia Review* 31, no. 1 (Spring 1977) (ABW).

"The Critic as Host", *Critical Inquiry* 3, no. 3 (Spring 1977) (CH).

"On Edge: The Crossways of Contemporary Criticism", *Bulletin of the American Academy of Arts and Sciences* 32, no. 4 (January 1979).

Fiction and Repetition: Seven English Novels (Cambridge: Harvard University Press, 1982) (FR).

"The Search for Grounds in Literary Study", *Genre* 17, nos. 1–2 (Spring-Summer, 1984) (SG).

The Linguistic Moment: From Wordsworth to Stevens (Princeton: Princeton University Press, 1985) (LM).

"Impossible Metaphor: Wallace Stevens's 'The Red Fern' as Example", *The Lesson of Paul de Man, Yale French Studies* 69 (1985).

The Ethics of Reading (New York: Columbia University Press, 1987) (ER).

Defacing It:
Hawthorne and History

For now we see through a glass, darkly; but then face to face.

1 Cor. 13:12

Ce qui arrive de par l'écriture n'est pas de l'ordre de ce qui arrive. Mais alors qui te permet de prétendre qu'il arriverait jamais quelque chose comme l'écriture? Ou bien l'écriture ne serait-elle pas telle qu'elle n'aurait jamais besoin d'advenir?

Maurice Blanchot[1]

What is the present relation between literary theory and pedagogy in American colleges and universities? Many professors of literature still assume that their chief responsibility is teaching students how to read "primary texts". The context in which that duty is performed, however, has changed radically from what it was thirty years ago. The old consensus in literary studies in the United States, such as it was, has been challenged in manifold ways. Widespread disagreement exists now about just what those "primary" texts ought to be and about just how they ought to be organized in courses and curricula. At the same time, as everyone knows, there has been a spectacular proliferation of powerful and incompatible "critical theories": structuralist, semiotic, Lacanian, Marxist, feminist, reader response, deconstructionist, new historicist, and so on.

In such a situation the relation of "theory" to "example" is fundamentally changed. Also changed is the relation of theory to the act of reading that example. In addition, the relation of that whole process to what may be called, by a kind of shorthand, "history" has changed. "History" here means something assumed to be radically different from either theory or literary texts – the real world of flesh-and-blood men and women living their daily lives, either in the past or now, when "history is being made every day".

All reading and teaching of literature is theoretical in the sense that it presupposes assumptions about what literature is and how it should be read. The difference now is that for complex reasons these assumptions need to be thought through and made overt. I mean by "literary theory" the shift from the hermeneutical process of identifying the meaning of a work of literature to a focus on the question of how that meaning is generated. When there is a general consensus about literary theory, if there ever was such a time (for example in that mythical time at the beginning of the present epoch of literary studies when the "new criticism" was more or less universally accepted in the United States), theory tends to be effaced, latent, presupposed. One just goes to work doing or teaching "close reading". When a multitude of conflicting critical theories call for attention, and when in addition there is confusion over the canons and the curricula of literature, as at the present time, then literary theory, rather than being something that can more or less be taken for granted, becomes overt, exigent, even, some would say, strident. Theory tends to become a primary means of access to the works read. These works now tend to be redefined as "examples" demonstrating the productive effectiveness of this or that theory. In such a situation, literary theory even tends to become a primary object for study in itself, as in that ever-increasing number of courses and programs these days in critical theory as such, sometimes treated historically, sometimes as a matter of current concern.

The "examples" read, at the same time, are no longer so often drawn from an established canon arranged in traditional canonical ways, for example by genre and historical period. The result is that the examples are likely to be subordinated to theory in the sense that the example is read as a more or less arbitrary choice among innumerable possible ones of a theoretical concept that claims universal applicability. The teacher teaches the student to read the example in a certain way, and the implicit claim is that everything should be read analogously. What is taught is a universal way of reading and its accompanying explicit theory, not the works of an agreed-upon canon read in canonical ways as having established meanings and as transmitting from the past agreed-upon cultural values. The place of those established meanings and enshrined values is more and more taken by theory itself.

Seen from this perspective, the function of theory is to liberate us from ideology, even from the ideology of theory itself. Critical theory performs an ethical and political act. It has institutional and social force. Critical theory is, then, no longer "merely theoretical". Rather, it makes something happen. It does this by disabling the power of the works read to go on proliferating the ideology that traditional canonical or thematic readings of them have blindly asserted. Critical theory, seen from this point of view, earns its label of "critical". It becomes within our educational institutions one of the most powerful and indispensable means of unmasking ideological assumptions.

All this seems clear enough and evident enough as a description of the present situation in literary studies. Each of the terms I have introduced, however, not only "ideology" itself, of course, but "theory", "example", "reading", and, especially, these days, "history", must by no means be taken for granted as transparent concepts whose meanings we already know. We would be unwise to take these received opinions as the basis for getting on with the business of reading literature, teaching it, writing about it. Each of these terms, especially "history", is deeply problematic, a question rather than an answer, perhaps even an unanswerable question.

It does not go without saying that we know at the beginning just what "critical theory" is. Moreover, there is reason to believe that there is no such thing as a *pure* theoretical statement. Even the most abstract and universal theoretical formulation will contain some indication of the range of examples to which it is meant to apply, or which might be used to test it. This is even the case with the claim that the theoretical formulation would be true of all texts whatsoever, written anywhere at any time in any language.

As for "example", no choice of examples is entirely arbitrary or innocent. The choice of an example may beg the very theoretical question it is meant to keep open. The problematic of example is the problematic of synecdoche, a vexed and obscure trope if there ever was one, squeezed as it is between metaphor and metonymy. A synecdochic example tends to be taken simultaneously as like the indeterminate whole of which it is a part and as merely one contingent part of a heterogeneous whole. Moreover, there is empirical reason to believe that the best examples in the great theoretical texts of the human sciences, both in philosophy and in literary criticism, are the severe displacement of theory rather than its triumphant confirmation.

"Reading", my third term, sounds like something we all understand, but a moment's reflection will show that nothing is more controversial these days than the question of just what it means to read a text, really to read it, that is, as opposed to passing its words through your mind. There is reason to fear, moreover, that reading in any of its senses takes place far less often than one might believe or wish.

"History", finally, as everyone knows, is often invoked these days as the sovereign antidote to the abstractions, the jargon, and the wild speculations of "theory". Such affirmations often seem to assume that we already know what history is. In fact nothing is more needed today than a prolonged, patient, scrupulous, and rigorous investigation of what is meant by a "historical happening", not to speak of the relation of literature to such happenings. One of the great benefits of the current "return to history" is the way the need for that investigation may again become apparent here and there.

This essay ends with a return to this issue in the light of the results of reading "The Minister's Black Veil". I have taken Hawthorne's story as a test case for theoretical formulations about realism and allegory proposed by Hawthorne himself and by his reader Henry James.

The interrogation of my four terms can, I claim, only be carried on by the exploration of an example. The example is somewhat arbitrarily chosen, according to the procedure I have already mentioned as characterizing our situation today. In order to interrogate the terms and their sequence I must follow the procedure I mean to interrogate. In what follows I shall try to initiate that questioning by way of Hawthorne's story, with some of its attendant documents: Hawthorne's prefaces to his stories and Henry James's book on Hawthorne. The example I have chosen is canonical. "The Minister's Black Veil" is read not only in advanced undergraduate and graduate courses in American literature, but also in introductory courses to literature both at the high school level and at the freshman or sophomore level in college courses.[2]

In the trajectory taken by the essay, an initial laying out of the opposition between realism and allegory as it is formulated by Hawthorne and James is followed by a reading of one example of this opposition, Hawthorne's story. Hawthorne and James set realism against allegory in a way that has a long genealogy before and after for Western speculation about the nature of literature. This opposition also has a specific importance within the tradition of American literature. The reading of the story culminates in the double proposition that the story is the unveiling of the possibility of the impossibility of unveiling. The initial theoretical hypothesis of an incompatibility between realism and allegory is erased by the actual reading. It is replaced by the proposition that both realism and allegory come to the same thing. Both are enigmatic and ultimately indecipherable narrative expressions of a strange kind of outside that resides inside and contaminates that inside. This "outside" can by no procedures of language be given an other than enigmatic expression. The proposition is expressed, in terms appropriate for "The Minister's Black Veil", as a simultaneous unmasking of the trope of prosopopoeia and recognition of its ineluctable reaffirmation in the very terms used to unmask it, for example in the word "unmask".

That formulation, in turn, of the outcome of the reading of the example, leads to concluding investigations of the claim that the act of writing "The Minister's Black Veil", or the act of reading it, wherever and whenever that reading takes place, are paradigmatic examples of an historical event as such. Identification of important consequences of this for the relations between theory and pedagogy end the essay.

Well known is the extraordinary passage in Henry James's *Hawthorne* (1879) presenting a litany of the things missing from American civilization that make it almost impossible for an American to write good novels:

> The negative side of the spectacle on which Hawthorne looked out, in his contemplative saunterings and reveries, might, indeed, with a little ingenuity, be made almost ludicrous; one might enumerate the items of high civilization, as it exists in other countries, which are absent from the texture of American life, until it should become a wonder to know what was left. No state, in the European

sense of the word, and indeed barely a specific national name. No sovereign, no court, no personal loyalty, no aristocracy, no church, no clergy, no army, no diplomatic service, no country gentlemen, no palaces, no castles, nor manors, nor old country-houses, nor parsonages, nor thatched cottages nor ivied ruins; no cathedrals, nor abbeys, nor little Norman churches; no great Universities nor public schools – no Oxford, nor Eton, nor Harrow; no literature, no novels, no museums, no pictures, no political society, no sporting class – no Epsom nor Ascot! . . . The natural remark, in the almost lurid light of such an indictment, would be that if these things are left out, everything is left out. The American knows that a good deal remains; what it is that remains – that is his secret, his joke, as one may say.[3]

Less well known than this splendid lament for the thinness of American culture are adjacent passages in which James specifies the double result of this deprivation in Hawthorne's writing. On the one hand, says James, there is an extraordinary poverty and literalism in Hawthorne's notebooks. The notebooks present a series of absolutely insignificant events:

He rarely takes his Note-Book into his confidence or commits to its pages any reflections that might be adapted for publicity; the simplest way to describe the tone of these extremely objective journals is to say that they read like a series of very pleasant, though rather dullish and decidedly formal, letters, addressed to himself by a man who, having suspicions that they might be opened in the post, should have determined to insert nothing compromising. . . . [The picture of America the reader constructs from these Notebooks] is characterized by an extraordinary blankness – a curious paleness of colour and paucity of detail. . . . We are struck by the large number of elements that were absent from [his circumstances], and the coldness, the thinness, the blankness, to repeat my epithet, present them-

selves so vividly that our foremost feeling is that of com-
passion for a romancer looking for subjects in such a field.
(J, 350–351)

James's figure here of a man writing a letter to himself
has extraordinary comic resonance. A letter to myself is
always in a sense totally blank, since it conveys no information that both sender and receiver do not already have,
both being the same person. But even a letter from myself
to myself, like those post cards discussed and manifested
in Derrida's *La Carte Postale*, is an "open letter", liable to
be "opened in the post". It therefore must be kept blank
if I am to preserve my privacy. Either way, such a letter
is blank, and such blankness, according to James, characterizes Hawthorne's notebooks. They present senseless,
uninterpreted factual detail, recorded in banal literalism,
as in the examples James cites: the man who falls through
an old log-bridge while out raspberrying, or the dog chasing
its tail,[4] or a whole paragraph given to the following: "The
aromatic odor of peat-smoke, in the sunny autumnal air is
very pleasant" (J, 352–353).
   On the other hand, according to James, Hawthorne has
a fatal tendency to fall into the abstraction of allegory. His
example of this is a famous passage in *The Scarlet Letter*
that, says James, really goes too far. It is the passage
describing Arthur Dimmesdale, Hester Prynne, and little
Pearl standing together at night on the scaffold. James
quotes it, and then comments:

That is imaginative, impressive, poetic; but when, almost
immediately afterwards, the author goes on to say that "the
minister looking upward to the zenith, beheld there the
appearance of an immense letter – the letter A – marked
out in lines of dull red light", we feel that he goes too far
and is in danger of crossing the line that separates the
sublime from its intimate neighbour. We are tempted to
say that this is not moral tragedy, but physical comedy. In

the same way, too much is made of the intimation that Hester's badge had a scorching property, and that if one touched it one would immediately withdraw one's hand. Hawthorne is perpetually looking for images which shall place themselves in picturesque correspondence with the spiritual facts with which he is concerned, and of course the search is of the very essence of poetry. But in such a process discretion is everything, and when the image becomes importunate it is in danger of seeming to stand for nothing more serious than itself. (J, 408)[5]

There would be much to say about these admirable passages. It would come down to saying that James indicts Hawthorne for dissolving the distinction between realism and allegory by producing images in either mode that are thin, blank, insignificant, and stand in the end for nothing more serious than themselves, like a letter written by a man to himself. Or, to put this another way, James reproaches Hawthorne for failing to make the material base in his stories, for example the actual piece of black crape in "The Minister's Black Veil", the fit vehicle for the allegorical meaning it is meant to carry. The discrepancy between vehicle and meaning manifests itself in the form of the unintentionally ludicrous. No doubt James was expressing indirectly his sense of his own problem as a young, ambitious American novelist. How could he rival Balzac or George Eliot with such impoverished materials? We know James's solution: to make the contrast and interaction between Americans and Europeans the chief topic of his novels.

Hawthorne stayed for the most part with American subjects (though not in *The Marble Faun* or "Rappaccini's Daughter"), but James's double diagnosis of the problems that resulted for him from doing this had already been made repeatedly by Hawthorne himself. This occurs especially in the admirable prefaces to his various collections of short stories and in the splendid comic piece of auto-analysis in the prefatory note to "Rappaccini's Daughter": "From the Writings of Aubépine". In these prefaces Hawthorne yields to the desire many writers have no doubt felt, the desire to write their own reviews, to do justice to themselves at last. But Hawthorne cannot resist turning this chance to praise himself into the reverse, a devastating critique of his own shortcomings.

Aubépine of course means "hawthorn" in French. The ironically wistful prefatory note to "Rappaccini's Daughter" imagines that Hawthorne's works have been written and published first in French. Now one of them, *Béatrice; ou la Belle Empoisonneuse*, is being published in English translation for the first time, as "Rappaccini's Daughter", with a prefatory note. Hawthorne here allows himself the pleasure of writing a little critical essay on his own work. It is unsparing in its analysis. The writings of M. de l'Aubépine, says this imaginary critic, "are not altogether destitute of fancy and originality; they might have won him greater reputation but for an inveterate love of allegory, which is apt to invest his plots and characters with the aspect of scenery and people in the clouds, and to steal away the human warmth out of his conceptions".[6] Just what Hawthorne means by "allegory" may not be all that easy to determine, but it is clearly opposed to "human warmth". Presumably the latter means something like the realistic portrayal of everyday life either of today or in history. Allegory presumably means the expression of some abstract meaning by way of the story. In Hawthorne's self-analysis the two goals of storytelling are irreconcilably opposed. You can do one or the other, but not both at once. "Allegory" has a remorseless power of disembodiment. It dissolves the solidity of realistic representation and makes it seem the picturing of cloud-cuckoo land.

This lament for his inability to bring together realism and allegorical meaning echoes through all Hawthorne's prefaces to his volumes of short stories. The "Preface" to *Mosses from an Old Manse* merits extended analysis. The whole extraordinary extended meditation focuses, however, on Hawthorne's fundamental problem as a writer: the irreconcilability of spiritual meaning and material embodiment. One example of this is Hawthorne's assertion that he moved into the old manse in the hope that he might write a substantial work there, a solid book incarnating spiritual wisdom. Hawthorne oddly emphasizes the materiality of the genuine book, its ability not only to have profound meaning but to take its independent place as a physical product of worth: "Profound treatises of morality; – a layman's unprofessional, and therefore unprejudiced view of religion; – histories, . . . bright with picture, gleaming over a depth of philosophic thought; – these were the works that might fitly have flowed from such a retirement. In the humblest event, I resolved at least to achieve a novel, that should evolve some deep lesson, and should possess physical substance enough to stand alone" (1124).

Though a novel is less substantial than a book of history, religion, or theology, it might take its place beside these if, strangely enough, it could attain physical solidity. Surely a book, however shallow its contents, has a substantial physical presence, if its author can get it printed. A book is a physical object like any other. It is able to stand alone, to hold up other books, or other furniture. It can even be used as a missile, and a booklover would do well to remember the sad story of the scholar who was crushed to death when a wall of his own books fell on him.

For Hawthorne, however, things do not seem to be so simple. Only if the *contents*, as one says, of the book, the meanings contained within its covers, are substantial, only if they have intellectual worth as valuable spiritual currency, can the book stand alone. If those meanings are insubstantial, they have a strange power to dissolve even the physical substance of the book and make it disembodied, ghostly. The book becomes a kind of phantom volume without volume, unable to stand alone. This is just what happens in Hawthorne's own case: "The treasure of intellectual gold, which I hoped to find in our secluded dwelling, had never come to light. No profound treatise of ethics – no philosophic history – no novel, even, that could stand, unsupported, on its edges" (1148). Instead of the solid work he hoped for, Hawthorne has written frail and insubstantial sketches that cannot stand alone.

These works suffer from a double powerlessness. On the one hand they do not communicate the secret mind and heart of Hawthorne to his readers. He remains as solitary as ever: "How little have I told! – and, of that little, how almost nothing is tinctured with any quality that makes it exclusively my own! . . . So far as I am a man of really individual attributes, I veil my face" (1147). Readers of "Wakefield", or of "The Christmas Banquet", or of many other Hawthorne stories, will know how central to his work is the theme of the incommunicability of selfhood. Gervayse Hastings, the anti-hero of "The Christmas Banquet", is one of those strange people who is "outside of everything [an extraordinary phrase!]; and nothing wearies the soul more than an attempt to comprehend them within its grasp" (867). The soul is wearied because the attempt, however hard it is made, is unsuccessful. Someone who is really "outside of everything" is also outside of language. Such a person remains as cold, as distant, as unapproachable as ever even after the most extravagant efforts to tell his or her story.

For Hawthorne, so it seems, subjectivity is, or can be, "outside of everything", perhaps even outside itself, or beside itself. If it is outside of everything, this means that it cannot touch anything closely enough to make that "anything" when it is named even a metonymic expression of itself, much less a metaphorical or symbolic expression giving access to the secret self by way of a similarity. One devastating form of this is the inability of a work of literature to function as a communication to others of the self of its author. Hawthorne is by no means sure that he even ought to try to communicate his secret selfhood. One's inner self may be that one thing of which one should not even try to speak. But even if he decides to try to reveal himself to his readers, he ends up not expressing himself but only appealing to "no sentiment or sensibilities, save such as are diffused among us all" (1147). He can express what everyone knows and feels, but not what he alone knows and feels. Hawthorne's way of saying this, his statement that insofar as he is individual he "veils his face", finds its unfolding, its explication and commentary, in "The Minister's Black Veil". Here I want to stress that there are two not entirely symmetrical binary oppositions at work in what Hawthorne says about the failure of his work.

On the one hand there is an opposition between realism and allegory. Only if the work is substantial, a thick object able to stand the sunlight and stand in the sunlight, will it be able to be the carrier of profound spiritual meaning and have that sort of meaning a work of philosophy, history, or theology possesses. In the case of storytelling, however it may be with history, philosophy, or theology, the two necessitites seem incompatible, mutually annihilating, at least in Hawthorne's experience of an attempt to combine the two. That opposition between banal truth-telling and outrageous disembodied allegory, noted by James, was diagnosed by Hawthorne himself as a fatal division undermining all his efforts as a writer. He can have the trivial but nevertheless historically substantial recording of the man falling off the bridge or of the dog chasing its tail, or he can have the great letter A in the sky, but he cannot seem to get the two sorts of meaning together.

On the other hand, Hawthorne suffers from another quite different opposition (at least apparently quite different). This is the incompatibility between expressing his own individuality and communicating anything at all. Even if he could succeed in embodying his secret selfhood in words, they would not be legible to others. If he can be understood it is because he expresses what his readers already know. Hawthorne somewhat ruefully boasts of the "sketches" in *Twice-told Tales* that: "They have none of the abstruseness of idea, or obscurity of expression, which mark the written communications of a solitary mind with itself. They never need translation. It is, in fact, the style of a man of society. Every sentence, so far as it embodies thought or sensibility, may be understood and felt by anybody, who will give himself the trouble to read it, and will take up the book in a proper mood" (1152). What Hawthorne here defines as the triumph, such as it is, of his tales and sketches is at the same time their failure. They do not need "translation", that is, the sort of commentary an allegory or a parable requires, a transformation of the realistic details of the story into the occult meanings those details carry. Anyone can read them. They do not need translation because they only tell their readers what those readers already know. But the whole aim of storytelling is to achieve this apparently impossible "translation", to translate, that is, the secret solitude and incommunicability of selfhood into terms that can be understood by others, or, in the alternative formulation, to express profound intellectual meanings, such as books of history, philosophy, or theology contain, in the solid embodiment of a realistic story about people like ourselves.

This second powerlessness of Hawthorne's tales and sketches, their inability to express profound intellectual meaning, is in a way even worse than their inability to express Hawthorne's hidden selfhood. His fragile and evanescent fabrications do not even succeed in expressing their own impersonal selves. They are "idle weeds and withering blossoms [no doubt hawthorn blossoms!] . . . old faded things, reminding me of flowers pressed between the leaves of a book" (1148–1149). Hawthorne's stories seem, in fact, at any moment liable to dissolve into nonsense or even to fade away altogether. The preface to "Rappaccini's Daughter" imagines the reviewer of "the writings of Aubépine" to say of them that "if the reader chance to take them in precisely the proper point of view, [they] may amuse a leisure hour as well as those of a brighter man; if otherwise, they can hardly fail to look excessively like nonsense" (975). Presumably he means that they look like nonsense because they are evidently intended to express an allegorical meaning that they fail utterly to "translate" into terms that make that meaning accessible to the reader. This is an amazing thing for a writer to say about his own work!

Even stranger is what Hawthorne says of that work in the preface to *Twice-told Tales*, the volume that includes "The Minister's Black Veil". There he first restates in its most succinct formulation the self-condemnation of his works as being fast fading blossoms in which realism is dissolved by allegory: "They have the pale tint of flowers that blossomed in too retired a shade – the coolness of a meditative habit, which diffuses itself through the feeling and observation of every sketch. Instead of passion, there is sentiment; and, even in what purport to be pictures of actual life, we have allegory, not always so warmly dressed in its habiliments of flesh and blood, as to be taken into the reader's mind without a shiver" (1151–1152). Read my tales and sketches, Hawthorne promises, and you will freeze to death. I guarantee it.

But worse follows just after, in the most hyperbolic condemnation of all. My pages, says Hawthorne, can only be read by twilight, where a half light partially illuminates the cave of subjectivity. In the full sun my books show themselves to be objects all right, but pure senseless objects, blank paper good only for wrapping fish or starting a fire: "The book, if you would see anything in it, requires to be read in the clear, brown, twilight atmosphere in which it was written; if opened in the sunshine, it is apt to look exceedingly like a volume of blank pages" (1152, and see the preface to *Mosses*, 1147, for the image of the mouth of the cave of subjectivity).

Strange self-analysis this, for a man who is one of the canonical classics of American literature. If Hawthorne is right about himself, we may be putting blank pages in the hands of all those high school and college students who are asked to read Hawthorne as one of the chief authors of our literature. No doubt there is some ironic denegation involved in Hawthorne's self-deprecation: "I know this is what people will say about my stories, so I'll say it for them first. In fact my stories are of inestimable value, as my readers would see if they were not such clods". Nevertheless, the other side of the irony no doubt is affirmed too, the side that asks to be taken straight. What Hawthorne says of himself, moreover, is just what James, apparently without irony, says of him, what some other expert readers, for example R. P. Blackmur in the Afterword to a Signet paperback selection of his tales,[7] have said, and no doubt what some of those not always willing student readers have mutely felt.

Is there any substance to what these readings and self-readings say about Hawthorne's lack of substance? If so, why is this? Why is it that Hawthorne's works, in the end, are, when seen in the full light of the sun, so many blank pages? A close look at one of the most canonical of the lot, "The Minister's Black Veil", may give some answers. Hawthorne's prefaces and James's book about Hawthorne have presented forcefully a theory of the incompatibility of realism and allegory within the conditions of American culture. A reading of one or more of his works would seem to be the best way to put that theory to the test. It is a good example of that peculiar relation between theory and reading I began this essay by identifying.

"The Minister's Black Veil"[8] is put by Hawthorne not under the aegis of the opposition between allegory and substantial realism, but within the space of a somewhat different contradiction. This is the opposition between the genres of parable and apocalypse, on the one hand, and true history, on the other.

The subtitle of the story is "A Parable". Though this

generic clue is not explicity followed up in the story itself, the subtitle invites the reader to figure out what it might mean to say that "The Minister's Black Veil" is a parable, that is, a realistic story that has a hidden spiritual meaning not necessarily made explicit within the story itself.

The word "veil" in the main title, however, points the reader in the direction of apocalypse. The word "apocalypse" means, etymologically, "unveiling". This association with apocalypse is reinforced by many details within the story. Like St John in *Revelation*, for example, the good Reverend Hooper keeps promising an imminent revelation. "There is an hour to come", he says to his financée, Elizabeth, "when all of us shall cast aside our veils . . . Be mine, and hereafter there shall be no veil over my face, no darkness between our souls! It is but a mortal veil – it is not for eternity!" (378, 379).

An initial footnote, on the other hand, a footnote to the word "parable" in the subtitle, gives the reader a historical original for the Reverend Mr Hooper, while at the same time taking away the explanatory force of that source in the very act of proffering it:

> Another clergyman in New England, Mr Joseph Moody, of York, Maine, who died about eighty years since, made himself remarkable by the same eccentricity that is here related of the Reverend Mr Hooper. In his case, however, the symbol had a different import. In early life he had accidentally killed a beloved friend; and from that day till the hour of his own death, he hid his face from men. (371)

To speak of "good parson Hooper" as "another clergyman of New England" encourages the reader to think of Hooper too as a historically real person. The circumstantiality of sociological detail in the story reinforces that. The story is firmly placed in a real town, Milford, Connecticut. Much effort is spent in making the story seem true to the life there, not "invested with the aspect of scenery and

people in the clouds". Nevertheless, the knowing reader
of Hawthorne at the same time realizes that the Reverend
Hooper is imaginary. Have we not already been told that
we are about to read "a parable"? And was the Reverend
Joseph Moody of York, Maine, a historical person, or has
Hawthorne invented him to create one of those spurious
historical originals of which there are many examples in
the history of fiction?[9]

Moreover, the veil worn by the Reverend Hooper's historical "original" had a specific, identifiable meaning, at
least according to Hawthorne. Everyone knew why Moody
wore the veil. He had accidentally killed a beloved friend.
In Hooper's "case, however, the symbol had a different
import." What import? That is just the question. This
question obsesses all Hooper's parishioners. It obsesses the
reader too. It is the one question worth asking and worth
answering about this story. What does the minister's black
veil *mean*? It is also the one question neither Hooper nor
Hawthorne will answer in so many words. Hawthorne in
effect says, "Read the story and figure it out for yourself."

In this Hawthorne is faithful to the genre of the parable.
With a parable it is always the case that if you understand
it you will not need to have it explained to you, whereas
if you are one of those who "have eyes and see not, ears
that neither hear not understand", all the explanation in the
world will not put you inside the meaning. Nevertheless, a
reading of the story, in the sense of a commentary such as
this one, promises just that, to provide an explanation that
will put its reader inside the story. This transgression
occurs in obedience to a regular law according to which a
parable simultaneously forbids commentary and demands
it. A literary critic is always damned if he does and damned
if he doesn't. An especially shrewd case of that occurs when
the critic yields to the temptation to provide an explanation
for a parable, in face of the fact that the definition of a
parable is that it expresses in a little story a meaning that
can be expressed in no other way.

Well, let us read the story and figure it out for ourselves, in the teeth of the prohibition against doing so. Or, rather, let me read the story for you and see if I can figure it out in a way that will "translate" from the text, through my commentary, to you my reader, this one of those fragile tales that Hawthorne says "never need translation". Perhaps they never need translation because they present nothing to translate. This might be either because they are so perspicuous as to be comprehensible to everyone or because they are so obscure that they are, when seen in the sunlight of common day, so many blank pages. My transgression of Hawthorne's prohibition against translation presupposes that in fact there *is* something to translate.

It is easy to say, "Let's read the story", or "Let me read the story for you", but what, exactly, would that act of translation mean? How would one know when one was in the presence of a real reading? *Reading* in one sense means passing the words of a text through one's mind and letting the words form meanings there. Nothing is easier or in a sense more passive. If you know the language and encounter something written in that language, say an advertising sign, you cannot not read it. The reading occurs automatically, by a kind of fatality, as when Tess in Hardy's *Tess of the d'Urbervilles* reads, in spite of herself, the sign in red letters being painted on a barn by an itinerant religious man: THOU SHALT NOT COMMIT . . . On the other hand, by "reading" in the sense of "translation" or commentary we mean something else, a transfer or carrying over of the meanings in the text to a language more conceptual, more general. And the carrying over, we assume, will be governed by some hermeneutical grasp or foreknowledge of the principle of coherence that holds the work together and makes it a whole.

How would one know when that carrying over had been done completely and successfully? Would every sentence, phrase, and word, even every syllable or letter, need "trans-

lation", as would surely be the case with a literal translation, or can commentary as translation work safely by
some synecdochic selection of part for whole that says,
"Trust me; the rest of it is just like this part of it I have
singled out"? How would one know that an exhaustive,
page by page, line by line, word by word, syllable by
syllable, letter by letter commentary was in fact exhaustive,
complete, not just a series of disconnected fragments without beginning, end, or principle of cohesion? Recognizing
and acknowledging this problem by no means constitutes
a solution to it. Every minuscule detail of "The Minister's
Black Veil" carries its weight of meaning and demands to be
"read" in the sense of glossed or translated, in a potentially
interminable commentary that the choice of a delimiting
topic or perspective by no means in the end curtails. The
curtailing is arbitrary, the implicit confession of fatigue or
the renouncing of an obligation. This obligation is generated by the text's demand to be "read", to find its adequate
commentary.

In saying, "Let me read for you 'The Minister's Black
Veil'", I make a promise, or I enter into a contract, an
alliance, a vow of faithfulness to report to you whatever
happens when I open my Hawthorne and begin to read the
words on the page. I promise to make that report with
absolute fidelity and to let the chips fall where they may,
even if what happens when I read is radically different
from what I expected would happen or what other commentaries had led me to expect would happen. To whom or to
what is that promise made? With whom or with what do
I sign a contract or promissory note, when I undertake to
fulfill an obligation to read? Who or what is the "I" who
signs such a contract and makes such a promise? Does not
a contract made with an impersonal text depersonalize the
one who signs the contract and make of him or her an
impersonal power of reading, of translating, and of relaying
to others what the text already relays? What the text already
relays is, in the case of "The Minister's Black Veil", that

of which this story is a parabolic expression, whatever *that* may be.

"The Minister's Black Veil" depends on a remarkable *donnée*, remarkable in its simplicity and profundity. It is a profundity that is all on the surface, or is accomplished by a change in marks all on the surface. The good Reverend Mr Hooper appears one Sunday at the door of his house to conduct the morning church service with "but one thing remarkable in his appearance" (372). He is wearing a black veil. He has covered over all but two of those features by which we ordinarily interpret a person's mind and feelings through his or her face. Hooper has replaced his face with another kind of mark. He has veiled his face.

No certain explanation is ever given, by the narrator, by Mr Hooper, or in any other way, of the reason or reasons he does this. His act is not related by him to his vocation as a minister, nor given explicit scriptural precedent, nor justified by other institutional precedents within his church, nor explained by a claim that he has been commanded to wear the black veil by God, or by his conscience, or by any other sort of message from on high or from out of this world. Such a message might have authorized him to wear the black veil as a sign transmitting that message, however enigmatically, to his community. Such explicit justifications for strange behavior by a claim to having a special mission or election are a familiar part of the history of Christianity, for example in the New England Puritanism that is the explicit historical reference of the story. Nor have they vanished today, when, for example, a TV Evangelist claims that "God will call him home" unless his followers donate several million dollars to his cause before such and such a day. Such explicit justifications are conspicuously absent from anything Hooper or the narrator or anyone else says about the reasons Hooper dons the black veil. In fact no explicit justification or explanation is ever given. This absence is itself a major clue to the right reading of the story.

Nor does the black veil itself, unlike the letter A in *The Scarlet Letter*, contain in itself any easily readable clues to its own meaning: "Swathed about his forehead, and hanging down over his face, so low as to be shaken by his breath, Mr Hooper had on a black veil. On a nearer view, it seemed to consist of two folds of crape, which entirely concealed his features, except the mouth and chin, but probably did not intercept his sight, farther than to give a darkened aspect to all living and inanimate things" (372). "A" stands for adultery, but black is more ambiguous. Certainly the story never says, in so many words, "Black stands for so and so". Black as such, moreover, is more the absence of signification than a clearly identifiable sign. The black veil is blank, featureless, except for its fold. It is remarkable in its absence of marks. What difference does it make that the veil is black rather than white or red? The reader is left to guess, primarily on the basis of universal associations of black with night-time, the absence of light, evil, death.

The black veil is double-folded. That seems as if it ought to be significant, but what does it signify? The story is silent on that point too. *The Minister's Black Veil* is one of the *Twice-told Tales*. The reader (this reader at least) is tempted to associate the doubling of the veil with the doubling of twice-telling. The story of the Reverend Hooper doubles the story of the Reverend Moody of York, Maine. Hawthorne's story makes its historical original twice-told. It might be argued that a twice-told tale, doubled back on itself, iterated, becomes through that iteration parabolic. All parables are twice-told, once as banal realism, once as deep allegorical significance. The folding of Hooper's black veil may express that.

The names may be significant. The Reverend Moody of York had reason to be moody, though this was in fact just

the name into which the historical Moody was born. He
had accidentally killed a beloved friend. The name Hooper
doubles or folds over the name Moody. It repeats the
double "o", already doubled itself in each name, like two
round eyes in the middle of each name. To change "M"
to "H" moves the name in the direction of Hawthorne's
own name. A "hooper" is either "a craftsman who fits the
hoops on casks, barrels, etc. a cooper. Also, a maker of
hoops", or "one who hoops or cries 'hoop'; only in *hooper's
hide*, an old name of hide-and-seek" (OED). The second
meaning comes from *hoop* in the sense of "to utter a hoop;
to whoop". Both of these meanings seem to "work". The
Reverend Hooper hoops himself within his veil, and, like
the hidden player who cries out in the game of hide-and-
seek, he speaks enigmatically from behind the veil: "Find
me if you can".

Nothing whatsoever along those lines, however, is said
in the story itself about the meaning either of the folding
or of the names. The reader is merely told that the veil
"seemed" to consist of two folds of crape, just as we are
told that it "probably" did not intercept his sight. The
names are just given as the proper names the two parsons
happened to have. It would be a courageous, not to say
foolhardy, commentator who would have the transgressive
temerity to say confidently just what the names mean, or
just what the double-folding of the black veil means, or
indeed even to explain just how it was folded, whether
horizontally or vertically, or how it was held on the good
Reverend Mr Hooper's face. The story is as silent about
the latter as it is about the typological meaning of the color
black or of the double folding. The reader might have it
right or might have it wrong. There is no way to tell for
sure, though much depends on getting it right, just as there
may be a severe penalty for getting it wrong.

"The Minister's Black Veil" is a little like the parables
of Jesus in the form modern biblical scholars tell us they
were almost certainly presented by Jesus himself, that is,

as enigmatic stories entirely lacking explicit interpretation. The latter were almost certainly added by the gospel-makers when they wrote down the story of Jesus's life a generation later. In the case of Hawthorne's story, though everyone involved – the narrator, Hooper's parishioners, Hooper himself, and the reader – are fascinated by the black veil and by the question of its meaning, no other than hypothetical explanations are ever given, even by Hooper himself. He tells his fiancée Elizabeth that "this veil is a type and a symbol", but when she asks in effect the natural next question, "Type and symbol of what?" or rather, to be specific, asks, "What grievous affliction hath befallen you . . . that you should thus darken your eyes for ever?" (378), he answers only in riddles and enigmas. He speaks in terms of "if" and "perhaps": "If it be a sign of mourning, . . . I, perhaps, like most other mortals, have sorrows dark enough to be typified by a black veil. . . . If I hide my face for sorrow, there is cause enough . . . and if I cover it for secret sin, what mortal might not do the same?" (378, 379).

Hooper begins his response to Elizabeth's challenge with his enunciation of the apocalyptic promise, already quoted. "Come, good sir", she says, "let the sun shine from behind the cloud. First lay aside your black veil; then tell me why you put it on." "There is an hour to come", he answers, "when all of us shall cast aside our veils. Take it not amiss, beloved friend, if I wear this piece of crape till then" (378). Hooper's iteration that we are all mortals associates the veil with the general condition of possible sin or possible sorrow that accompanies the certainty of death. To be mortal is to be veiled, or to have an obligation to be veiled. Only at the last trumpet, after death, in the general resurrection, will all the veils be removed at once. More is done in the story with these apocalyptic associations of veiling, and about those I shall have more to say. But they too are rather a matter of possibilities proffered in such a way that they are withdrawn at the moment they are put forth than a matter of clear identification of a delimited meaning for veiling as such. It is a characteristic of the apocalyptic promise that it is never fulfilled here and now. It is always a matter of imminence, of not quite yet. The apocalyptic speaker makes a promise that is always about to be fulfilled: "Watch, wait with me, for the end is at hand when all will be revealed".

The black veil covers all of Hooper's face but his mouth and chin. Much is made of the "sad smile" (374) that dimly glimmers beneath the Reverend Hooper's black veil. That smile is another sign, another textual clue to be read, but it too has no certain meaning. A sad smile is an oxymoron. It is neither happy nor sad, but both at once. A smile detached from the rest of the features of a human face is fundamentally ambiguous. It is not open to certain interpretation. It may mean this or it may mean that. It may mean Hooper is happy or it may mean he is sad. It is impossible to tell, since the meaning of a smile depends on its configuration with the other features of the face. These are in the Reverend Hooper's case invisible. He is in this like the Cheshire cat in *Alice in Wonderland*. That cat, you will remember, vanishes bit by bit until only its disembodied smile remains. "I have seen a cat without a smile", says Alice, "but never a smile without a cat." The good Reverend Mr Hooper has a smile without a face.

The glimmering of that sad smile associates it with the figurative system of sunshine, twilight, and darkness that is one of the pervasive clues to parabolic meaning presented by the text. Elizabeth, for example, says, "let the sun shine from behind the cloud". Hooper's dimly glimmering smile is like the sun in eclipse or behind a cloud. As the sun is the visible symbol or delegate of God, Hooper as the minister of his congregation is another such representative. He is the mediator between his parishioners and the kingdom of heaven. When Hooper appears in his black veil it is as though the sun had been suddenly covered by a cloud, or, even more alarmingly, as if it had been suddenly eclipsed, "like a sudden twilight in the air" (379). That Hooper should be in eclipse, mysteriously veiled, is far more threatening to the community than if an ordinary citizen were to cover his face.

This solar system of figures tends to include some reference to faces as well as to the sun, to darkness, and to veiling clouds. This system is pervasive in our tradition, both in Greek thought, most notoriously in Plato, as in the parable of the cave in *The Republic*, and in the Bible, for example in that passage from St Paul I have quoted as an epigraph to this essay, but also in the following passage from *Romans*: "The night is far spent, the day is at hand: let us therefore cast off the works of darkness, and let us put on the armour of light" (Rom. 13:12), or in the astronomical imagery of the book of *Revelation*, that great exemplar of apocalypse in our culture: "And there appeared a great wonder in heaven; a woman clothed with the sun, and the moon under her feet, and upon her head a crown of twelve stars" (Rev. 12:1). The sun in the sky is the delegated symbol of the One, for Plato, or of God Almighty, for the biblical and Christian tradition. As a source of light by which we see and identify objects and people, the sun has both an epistemological and an ethical significance. It is only because the sun has risen that Socrates in the *Protagoras* can see the face of Hippocrates and recognize that he is blushing in shame at wanting to become a sophist. To see right, for example to see correctly the faces of our neighbours, is both to identify accurately and to have moral insight. To dwell in darkness is both to be without knowledge and to be in moral error. Apocalypse promises the imminent end of darkness. It promises a general illumination when we shall see both God and our neighbour face to face in a general reciprocity of insight. This ultimate revelation is proleptically foreshadowed by any glad day of general sunshine and community celebration here in this subsolar world: "The night is far spent, the day is at hand."

Parable as a genre is like apocalypse in promising such a revelation or illumination, while at the same time deferring it. All the parables of Jesus have as their sole topic the good news about the kingdom of heaven and the right procedures for getting there. Kafka's *Von den Gleichnissen* ("On Parables") says parables promise a transformation of our lives in which we "go over" and "become parables" (whatever *that* means).[10] One difference between parable and apocalypse is that parable focuses more explicitly than apocalypse on the way the right reading of the parable itself causes a transformation, and on the way the almost universal failure to read the parable right is the sign of our distance from the final unveiling. According to the parables of Jesus, a chief way to get to the kingdom of heaven is to be a good reader of parables, or a good listener when they are presented orally, but most of us are among those who having eyes, see not, ears that neither hear not understand. The parable is therefore both the means of getting to the kingdom of heaven and the blocking agent forbidding access. If you do not already understand the parable, the parable itself is not going to help you understand it. My copy of the King James Bible marginally glosses seeing "through a glass, darkly" as meaning seeing "in a riddle". "In a riddle", the gloss says, is a more literal translation of the Greek original. Our veiled or darkened state is chiefly expressed in that the kingdom of heaven must for us be expressed parabolically, in a riddling form. It must be veiled or darkly glassed in "type and symbol", for example in the minister's black veil, rather than expressed directly. Only when we have crossed over will we be able to see unveiled, that is, face to face. To cross over into parable would be to be in that unthinkable and unsayable realm where there is no longer any distinction between literal and parabolic language, or, in Hawthorne's more usual terms, between history and allegory. We shall need no more types and symbols then. Our present situation is that of an indefinite suspension within the imminence of an end that could be brought about instantly and magically if we could read the types and symbols right and unveil what is hidden beneath them.

"The Minister's Black Veil" appropriates and reworks this system of thought and figure. The right reading of this reworking is a chief means of understanding the story, insofar as it can be understood. The story opens with a celebration of the happy openness and reciprocity of the Milford community. Everyone's face is open to his neighbour's face on this bright sunshiny Sunday at churchtime: "The old people of the village came stooping along the street. Children, with bright faces, tript merrily beside their parents, or mimicked a graver gait, in the conscious dignity of their Sunday clothes. Spruce bachelors looked sidelong at the pretty maidens, and fancied that the Sabbath sunshine made them prettier than on weekdays" (371). All the generations are here together with open faces in the sunshine: old folks, parents, children, courting unmarried citizens, that is, bachelors and maidens preparing for the marriages leading to new children with bright faces. It is almost as if the kingdom of heaven were already here on earth. It is almost as if the good people of Milford could already see not through a glass darkly but face to face.

Mr Hooper's appearance in his black veil at the door of his house for the short walk to preside over the Sunday service is a devastating eclipse of all that sunshine openness. It interrupts the universal process, necessary to all human society – community life, family life, and face to face "interpersonal" relations – whereby each of us interprets the countenances of those around us as signs of those persons' selfhoods. When the parson appears in his black veil, his soul, his thoughts, or his feelings, may no longer be read from his face. There is no way to tell whether he is happy, or whether he has a secret sorrow or sin. It is impossible to be sure the same person is in there, or any person at all. It may be a stranger's visage, product of some diabolical shifting or displacement: "'Are you sure it is our parson?' inquired Goodman Gray of the sexton . . . 'I can't really feel as if good Mr Hooper's face was behind that piece of crape,' said the sexton"; "They longed for a breath of wind to blow aside the veil, almost believing that a stranger's visage would be discovered, though the form, gesture, and voice were those of Mr Hooper" (371; 373). Something worse even than a stranger, a ghost or a demon, may be hidden behind the veil: "He has changed himself into something awful, only by hiding his face" (372); "The black veil, though it covers only our pastor's face, throws its influence over his whole person, and makes him ghost-like from head to foot" (374).

If prosopopoeia is the ascription of a name, a face, and a voice to the absent, the inanimate, or the dead, and if this trope is transferred from that universal act whereby we assume a person's face, voice, form, and figure are signs of the subjectivity of that person, good parson Hooper has put not the figurative but the originary literal version of this act of reading in doubt. He has done this by removing one of its essential elements, the face, though leaving the rest, the voice, gesture, form, figure, and name.

Hooper's veil also interrupts the process whereby each of us interprets himself in the same way, for example when we look in the mirror: "That is me there facing me from within the glass, the self I am for myself and the self I am for other people." If the black veil makes Hooper "awful" to his neighbours, he also becomes awful to himself. His attempt to wish happiness to the couple he has just married is broken when "catching a glimpse of his figure in the looking-glass, the black veil involved his own spirit in the horror with which it overwhelmed all others. His frame shuddered – his lips grew white – he spilt the untasted wine upon the carpet – and rushed forth into the darkness" (376). Later the narrator tells the reader that Hooper felt "that a preternatural horror was interwoven with the threads of the black crape. In truth, his own antipathy to the veil was known to be so great, that he never willingly passed before a mirror, nor stooped to drink at a still fountain, lest, in its peaceful bosom, he should be affrighted by himself" (380). The black veil hides Hooper from himself, as he thinks he has access to that self by looking at his own face in the mirror.

One of Hawthorne's frequent names for the hidden self is "heart". Hooper's wearing of the black veil, says the narrator, "kept him in that saddest of all prisons, his own heart" (382). When Ethan Brand, in Hawthorne's story of that name, has been purified into lime in his own limekiln, what remains is a skeleton of lime and a lump of lime in the shape of a human heart. All Brand's flesh can be burned away, but his heart remains, that material embodiment of the secrecy of consciousness, hidden even from itself. The unpardonable sin, it may be, that Ethan Brand seeks all through the world and finds ultimately at home in his own heart, is that unreachable secrecy of consciousness. This secrecy may in no way be given an outward, material embodiment making it communicable to others. A preternatural horror is interwoven with the threads of Hooper's veil, at least to Hooper's sense of it. This makes the veil, so it seems, an example of what Hawthorne has been seeking unsuccessfully in all his writing: the material embodiment of a spiritual or allegorical meaning. The "horror" woven into the physical threads of the crape, however, is the horror of the inaccessibility of what is behind the veil. It is the preternatural horror of unveiling the possibility of the impossibility of unveiling, even within or beyond the grave.

Hooper's veil also interrupts an important way in which we sustain our sense of ourselves. This is the way other people whose faces we can see look us in the face with signs of recognition. These looks affirm that we are familiar to those around us. This leads us to believe that we are who we think we are. One of the most disquieting effects of Hooper's wearing of the black veil is the way it puts in doubt his parishioners' sense of themselves. This has depended to a considerable degree on their feeling that they live under the benign fatherly eye of the good Reverend Mr Hooper. Now they cannot be sure whether he is looking at them or not, or indeed whether it is still Hooper at all behind the veil. "Lift the veil but once", implores Elizabeth, Hooper's fiancée, "and look me in the face" (379). Our sense of ourselves is determined in part by the fact that others look us in the face and affirm our sense of our own selfhood. The other who looks me and my neighbours in the face plays the role of the all-illuminating sun, or of God himself. The look of the paternal other brings each of us into visible or externalized existence and keeps us there by responding to our faces, smiles, frowns, and speech as valid signs that there is something behind our faces, that is, our real selves. The veiled face of the other is a terrifying or "awful" threat to that.

Hooper's appearance in his black veil interrupts even the way in which we interpret a dead body as the effigy of that person. A dead body is normally taken as the model or form of that person's departed soul, for example in the case of recumbent statues on tombs in medieval churches. We want to look the dead in the face, as in the ceremony of viewing the corpse, both to be sure that the dead are really dead and as a way of forming an image of what the dead must still be like in the realm of death to which they have now crossed over. The custom of viewing the dead is a way of personifying death, giving it a face, and thereby giving ourselves the courage to face it.

All the interchanges and transactions of ordinary social life – birth, courtship, marriage, going to church, discussions among citizens of matters of interest to the community, the ritual acceptance of death, and so on – depend on accepting the face as a trustworthy sign of the subjectivity within, readable as an index to that subjectivity by those who know how to read. All these transactions are interrupted, inhibited, or suspended when Hooper appears in his veil.

The effects on the community of Milford of this interruption are catastrophic. Everything presupposed by the cheerful picture of social harmony sketched in the opening paragraph breaks down. Hooper preaches from behind his black veil a sermon on "secret sin", the sin we would hide from our neighbours, from ourselves, and from God. The sermon causes the hearts of Hooper's parishioners to quake. When they leave the church they have been transformed, at least in the narrator's description, from faces open to one another in the sunlight into mouths without faces or into solitary selves, veiled in secret meditation: "Some gathered in little circles, huddled closely together, with their mouths all whispering in the centre; some went homeward alone, wrapt in silent meditation" (374).

The story thereafter is a series of episodes in which one by one the normal activities of the community are shown to be disabled, transformed, or suspended by Hooper's wearing the black veil: a funeral service, a wedding, consultation with the minister by members of his congregation, Hooper's open interchange with his fiancée, his customary evening walk to the graveyard, his power as a preacher, his own deathbed scene, even the thought of him after his death by those who survive him. Once the minister puts on his black veil there is no more open discussion, no more courtship, no more marrying or giving in marriage, or, rather, marriages become indistinguishable from funerals, and funerals cease to be an institutionalized acceptance of the fact that the dead are really dead.

It would seem the easiest thing in the world for Hooper's parishioners to ask him straight out what the black veil on his face means, "to put the plain question to Mr Hooper, wherefore he did this thing" (377). The presence of the veil itself, however, seems magically to forbid questions about it:

There was the black veil, swathed around Mr Hooper's forehead, and concealing every feature above his placid mouth, on which, at times, they could perceive the glimmering of a melancholy smile. But that piece of crape, to their imagination, seemed to hang down before his heart, the symbol of a fearful secret between him and them. Were the veil but cast aside, they might speak freely of it, but not till then. Thus they sat a considerable time, speechless, confused, and shrinking uneasily from Mr Hooper's eye, which they felt to be fixed upon them with an invisible glance. Finally, the deputies returned abashed to their constituents . . . (377)

If the veil were a third, so to speak, side by side with those in dialogue about it, if it were an object both interlocutors might look at and discuss, then it would not suspend the give and take of open speech. When it hangs between person and person, though it is still the same innocent piece of black crape, it puts an abrupt stop to dialogue. The veil stands as an impenetrable barrier between person and person. It functions as a formidable interdict against the face to face open discussion that is the basis of community interchange and consensus. How can there be a community unless its members can talk openly to one another and come by that free interchange to an agreement about political and ethical issues? The minister's black veil puts a stop to all that. Since he has sworn never to put it aside, the prohibition is a permanent postponement of a return to open dialogue. In this the veil is like the perpetual deferral inextricably woven into the apocalyptic promise. Now we see through a glass, darkly; but then face to face. But the "then" will never come within mortal time.

The Sunday when Mr Hooper preaches his first morning sermon swathed in his black veil occurs of course before the visit of the speechless deputation of Hooper's parishioners, just cited. On that first day he wears the veil

Hooper in the afternoon and evening conducts a funeral and then a wedding service. Far from being a peaceful laying of the dead in their graves, funerals conducted by the Reverend Hooper in his veil have a disquieting power of resurrection. When he stoops over the dead maiden to bid her farewell, "the veil hung straight down from his forehead, so that, if her eyelids had not been closed for ever, the dead maiden might have seen his face" (375). Only a dead face can now be permitted to look Hooper in the face, in anticipation of the apocalyptic unveiling after death Hooper keeps promising. Here and now, at the dead maiden's funeral, the dead and the living faces confront one another. As a superstitious old woman affirms, "at the instant when the clergyman's features were disclosed, the corpse had slightly shuddered, rustling the shroud and muslin cap, though the countenance retained the composure of death" (375). As the mourners walk behind the corpse to the graveyard, two of them have the impression that "the minister and the maiden's spirit were walking hand in hand" (376).

If a funeral becomes an uncanny resurrection as an effect of the veil, a wedding on the other hand becomes a funeral. If Hooper can as it were raise the dead, in his black veil he also has the contrary power to strike the living dead. It is as though he were a black sun emanating a power of blackness: "A cloud seemed to have rolled duskily from beneath the black crape, and dimmed the light of the candles. The bridal pair stood up before the minister. But the bride's cold fingers quivered in the tremulous hand of the bridegroom, and her death-like paleness caused a whisper, that the maiden who had been buried a few hours before, was come from her grave to be married. If ever another wedding were so dismal, it was that famous one, where they tolled the wedding-knell" (376).

In some sharp remarks, in response to an oral presentation of an earlier and shorter version of this essay, D. A. Miller stressed the sexual implications of Hooper's wearing of the veil. His remarks were sharp both in the sense of sharply critical and in the sense of having insight into Hawthorne's story. Miller recalled Poe's review of Hawthorne's *Twice-Told Tales*. There Poe asserts that the Reverend Hooper is clearly guilty of some unspeakable crime against a woman. The "*moral* put into the mouth of the dying minister", said Poe, is no more than a veil for its "insinuated" meaning, which is that "a crime of dark dye (having reference to the "young lady") has been committed".[11] D. A. Miller asserted that the story reflects, represents, or expresses the general historical situation, in nineteenth-century America and in the West generally at that time, of the repression and keeping secret of sexuality. "We have learned ", said Miller (who is this "we"?), "not just from the work of Michel Foucault, but also, no less pertinently, from the whole nineteenth-century tradition of Gothic and sensation fiction that culminates in Freud's case histories, how seamlessly our culture conjoins subjectivity, secrecy, and sexuality, each as the truth of the other. Modern subjectivity is most fundamentally imagined as the place of a privacy that is only guaranteed by the secrets that may be kept there, and these secrets are ritually specified – or, as the case may often be, ritually unspecified – with primary reference to the category of 'sexuality'".[12]

But surely, just because our culture "imagines" that, that does not mean that our culture has got it right. It may be that our culture uses the category of sexuality as a conveniently cathected veil, a focus of fascinated attention, to cover something else. "We" may be fooled into thinking we have performed an ultimate unveiling and cultural demystification when we triumphantly come forward with "sexuality", "sexual secrets", as the truth behind the veil or as the essential historical context that determines the meaning of the story. This is the interpretative move made by Miller in his discussion of "The Minister's Black Veil" and in his criticism of my reading.

Miller claimed that my "ontologizing" of the story and of the veil is a means of obscuring, and at the same time of exercising, administrative academic power. But surely such an identification of the "truth" of subjectivity as Miller makes when he says that truth is, in our culture, "sexuality", can be just as effective a means of policing and of social and educational administration as any other claim of interpretative authority. He would simply substitute one administrative power for another supposed one.

I should claim, in fact, that to call attention, as my reading of "The Minister's Black Veil" does, to the incommensurability of cause and effect in the social world, and to the relation of this to the possibility of the impossibility of unveiling, is to perform a more effective act of the putting in question of power than the spurious claim to have found the causative historical agent behind or beside the veil. My way of reading, I also assert, makes possible a more responsible exercise of administrative or educational power than D. A. Miller's. He accuses me of masking an authority by displacing it and neutralizing it. I have done in fact exactly the opposite. I have identified how Hawthorne shows the authority Hooper's donning of the veil gives him to be without authority, either transcendental or social. I have shown how Miller's reading is, in its making of sexual secrets an ultimate explanatory ground, another version of the metaphysics of unveiling he would contest. Much is at stake here, not least the question of whether the critic asserts authority over the text by claiming to know more than the text knows, as Miller does, or whether the critic grants authority to the text, an authority both cognitive and performative, as my reading does. At stake also is the role of historical contextualizing in asserting authority over a literary text.

Certainly the sexual implications of "The Minister's Black Veil" are important, for example in the veil itself, in the episodes of the funeral and the wedding, and in the stress on Hooper's relations to Elizabeth and to other women. But surely repressed sexuality is not an endpoint in the reading nor an ultimate ground of the text, the principle by which a total accounting for it may be given. What is repressed in repressed sexuality is something – that "we" only problematically call a "thing" – that can never by any means or in any conceivable social organization, be brought into the open, though the modes of that remaining hidden no doubt differ from one moment in history to another. What is repressed, hidden, or veiled when sexuality is veiled can never be uncovered. The lifting of a veil only reveals another veil behind, as Hawthorne's story "shows". There is just as much repression now, in a period of so-called sexual openness, as in more apparently "repressed" times, such as the nineteenth century. Sexuality is more an allegorical vehicle in Hawthorne's story for something else than a primary literal referent. Another way to put this is to say that sexual repression is not the effect of particular social apparatuses of organization, policing, or repression. Such modes of social control are rather inevitable concomitants (I do not say effects) of sexual repression. This sexual "repression" could not by any means or by any change in social organization be unrepressed, liberated, since it is a mode of something else more hidden even than sexual secrets, something far more deeply interfused, hidden but on the surface, like Hooper's black veil itself. That does not mean, of course, that so-called "sexual repression" does not manifest itself in quite different ways from one society to another or from one historical time to another in the same society, nor that efforts toward "sexual liberation" are not socially desirable. But it does mean that it would be a mistake to pin millennial hopes on such liberation.

Just what is that "something else"? Let me look more narrowly at the elements in "The Minister's Black Veil" having to do with sexual difference in order to approach a preliminary answer. But I need to move circumspectly here, to have prudence and patience.

No doubt part of the disquieting effect of Hooper's black veil lies in the fact that it is an ordinarily feminine article of clothing worn by a man. Hooper is a weird kind of transvestite, weird because wearing the veil by no means feminizes him nor even makes him sexually neutral. He remains aggressively masculine, patriarchal. He comes gradually to be known "throughout the New-England churches" as "Father Hooper" (381).

A woman who becomes a nun "takes the veil". The nun's veil is a symbol of her vow of perpetual virginity, her promise perpetually to cover her sex. The covering of the face serves as a displacement of the covering of the pudenda. A man who becomes a monk, on the other hand, is tonsured, a symbolic castration. Gerard Manley Hopkins, speaking of his vow of celibacy, but also of the associated inhibition of his creative powers, said, "I am a eunuch – but it is for the kingdom of heaven's sake."[13] A woman can wear a veil for other reasons, however, than as a sign she is a nun. A woman's veil may be a sign of widowhood. The widow's veil is a sign that her sex is now covered for good. St Paul says a woman should wear a veil in church as a sign of her inferiority to man (1 Cor. 11:3–15). A woman may wear a veil as an adornment on a hat, signifying no more than proper womanly modesty and reserve. The woman's veil is a displacement of her hymen. It expresses her sexual modesty or unavailability. Her veil is a screen before her sex. A woman who wears a veil asserts that she is the sort who keeps covered what ought to be kept covered. A veil on a woman's face is therefore perfectly proper. But when a man appropriates that expression of female *pudeur* it becomes improper, shocking, deeply unsettling. It becomes "terrible" in the sense of terrifying, as one of Hooper's female parishioners observes: "'How strange', said a lady, 'that a simple black veil, such as any woman might wear on her bonnet, should become such a terrible thing on Mr Hooper's face!'" (374).

On the other hand, the veil has not always been purely feminine in its connotations. In a discussion of the Hebrew word *gala*, Old Testament counterpart of the New Testament Greek word *apokálupsis*, Jacques Derrida observes that though both words mean unveiling, the Hebrew word is more directly associated with the act of uncovering parts of the body, the eyes or the ears, or the sex of either sex. He cites some odd passages in Leviticus, 20:11,21: "The man that lieth with his father's wife hath uncovered his father's nakedness", and "If a man shall take his brother's wife, it is an unclean thing: he hath uncovered his brother's nakedness."[14] What is odd about these passages is not the prohibition against specific forms of incest, but the strange formulation that makes the son who sleeps with his father's wife (who may not be his mother if his father has remarried) uncover not her nakedness, but his father's. The mother's or foster-mother's nakedness belongs to the father, and to uncover the mother is to uncover the father, just as to uncover the brother's wife is to uncover the brother. It is the act of unveiling in adultery, fornication, or incest that is the wicked thing. In these cases the wickedness is defined as an uncovering of male nakedness, or of male nakedness by way of female nakedness. Such acts uncover that which ought to remain covered, but the transgression may be either of a man's or of a woman's "nakedness". Both men and women should keep themselves properly veiled. The story of how Ham saw the "nakedness" of his drunken father, Noah, in Genesis 10:20–27, suggests that the unveiling of the male is an especial desecration.

In "The Minister's Black Veil" Hooper's relations to three different women are specified: the dead maiden for whom he performs the funeral service, the live maiden for whom he performs the wedding ceremony, later on the same day, and his fiancée Elizabeth. In all three cases the minister's black veil is a barrier between the two. The barrier is displaced in this case from the woman to the man. At the same time the veil is the means or the medium of a connection between the two "stronger than death", or lasting even beyond the grave. These passages in the text confirm that Poe was right to say that Hooper was guilty of "a crime of dark dye (having reference to the 'young lady')". Poe presumably meant by "young lady" Elizabeth, but Hooper commits that crime with all three maidens.

What was the crime? No doubt it was that transgression dear to Poe's own imagination, necrophilia. Hooper likes them dead. For him the only good woman is a dead woman, a woman, moreover, who has died still virgin. The only "person" who ever looks him in the face after he dons the veil is the dead maiden whose funeral he performs on the first day he appears in the veil. That "shudder" of the maiden's corpse when the clergyman's features are disclosed to her (or to "it"), in a passage already cited, can be seen as a sexual spasm as well as a sign of resurrection. The "fancy" two of the congregation have that they see the minister and the maiden's spirit walking hand in hand in the funeral procession images a union of the two beyond the grave. This union is solemnized when the minister in his black veil, in the next episode of the story, turns the living bride so pale that a whisper goes round the church that "the maiden who had been buried a few hours before, was come from her grave to be married" (376). "The Wedding-Knell", the story just previous to this one in *Twice-Told Tales*, is alluded to in this episode: "If ever another wedding were so dismal, it was that famous one, where they tolled the wedding-knell" (376). In "The Wedding-Knell", the aged bridegroom, able to marry his aged bride at last, after all her cruel postponements of their union, appears at the wedding in his shroud and bids the sexton toll the funeral knell for the wedding. Hooper's black veil too is a kind of shroud and makes of him a revenant from beyond the grave. For him sexual union can only appropriately take place beyond the infinite postponement of death.

This aspect of the veil returns most forcefully in Hooper's encounters with his fiancée Elizabeth. The deputation from the congregation is struck dumb by the sight of the veiled minister. They cannot speak out the reproach they have come to deliver. Elizabeth, on the other hand, asks him frankly to doff the veil: "Come, good sir, let the sun shine from behind the cloud. First lay aside your black veil: then tell me why you put it on"; "Lift the veil but once, and look me in the face" (378; 379). Elizabeth's invitation no doubt has a sexual implication. It is an invitation to that sort of unveiling that takes place, or ought to take place, only between husbands and wives: "As his plighted wife, it should be her privilege to know what the black veil concealed" (378). Hooper's response in effect widows her before she has been married by promising her a union that can only take place after death. Stick with me, he says, and I promise you a complete unveiling and a complete union after we are both dead, though the veil must come between us as long as we are alive: "Do not desert me, though this veil must be between us here on earth. Be mine, and hereafter there shall be no veil over my face, no darkness between our souls! It is but a mortal veil – it is not for eternity!" (379).

Both Elizabeth and Hooper are aware, in different ways, of the discrepancy between the veil as a mere double-folded piece of black crape, and the veil as "a type and a symbol" of each separate consciousness's secrecy, a secrecy that no sexual unveiling can expose. Elizabeth "could discern nothing of the dreadful gloom that had so overawed the multitude: it was but a double fold of crape, hanging down from his forehead to his mouth, and slightly stirring with his breath" (378). She refuses Hooper's offer of a marriage in which the separation of souls will be indicated by his still wearing the veil even at times of sexual union. Of this refusal the narrator comments: "Mr Hooper smiled to think that only a material emblem had separated him from happiness, though the horrors which it shadowed forth, must be drawn darkly between the fondest of lovers" (379–380).

Though Elizabeth rejects such a marriage, she remains unwed, secretly faithful to Hooper. She tends him on his deathbed, honoring his wish to remain veiled until death and even to be buried in his veil: "But in his most convulsive struggles, and in the wildest vagaries of his intellect, when no other thought retained its sober influence, he still showed an awful solicitude lest the black veil should slip aside. Even if his bewildered soul should have forgotten, there was a faithful woman at his pillow, who, with averted eyes, would have covered that aged face, which she had last beheld in the comeliness of manhood" (382).

Hawthorne's treatment of the sexual aspect of Hooper's wearing of the veil both expresses the nineteenth-century ideology associating the separateness of consciousness with sexuality and at the same time "deconstructs" that ideology. Hawthorne did not need to wait for Michel Foucault to teach him this association nor to teach him that it is an ideology, that is, the mistaking of a sign for a material reality. Hawthorne's deconstruction, woven into the textuality or material substance of the words of the text, takes two forms. On the one hand, he shows the belief that subjectivity is always the repository of sexual secrets to be inseparable from the religious ideology with which it is connected. Just as the Hebrew *gala* became the Greek *apokálupsis*, so Hooper's refusal of sexual union with Elizabeth is inextricably tied to his belief in a general unveiling at the last trumpet: "'There is an hour to come,' said he, 'when all of us shall cast aside our veils'". You cannot have the one ideology without the other. In our culture the ideology that says the secrecy of subjectivity, of the "I", is always primarily sexual is part of Western metaphysics.

Insofar as Hawthorne shows that version of our tradition called "New England Puritanism" to be a powerful, repressive, and socially destructive mystification, and insofar as he shows the notion of secret sexual sin to be part of that mystification, a story like "The Minister's Black Veil" works to unmask the sexual component of that ideology too, for those who have eyes to see and ears that can hear and understand.

On the other hand, Hawthorne deconstructs this ideology in another way: by showing repeatedly the way this ideology depends on fetishizing material symbols, in the case of "The Minister's Black Veil" that mere piece of doublefolded black crape. In all his work Hawthorne remains fascinated by the discrepancy between ideological value and the material base that value must always have. An example is the discrepancy between the Great Stone Face, in the story of that name, and the meaning the hero and his community invest in the face. The reader is told at the beginning that on a near approach the face reveals itself to be "only a heap of ponderous and gigantic rocks, piled in chaotic ruin one upon another" (1068), but that does not prevent the projection of a benign patriarchal presence into this heap of stones.

To say that the meaning of "The Minister's Black Veil" is determined by its reference to the repression of sexuality in the American culture of Hawthorne's day is to be mystified by the ideology that Hawthorne unmasks. It is to commit a double error: the error of believing that sexuality can be detached from the metaphysical and religious ideas that are woven into it, so made a separate area of social policing, and the age-old error of confusing cause with effect, effect with cause. In this case the metalepsis sees the social structure as the cause, when the latter is the effect of the ideological assumption that behind every veil is a sexual crime, some *gala* or uncovering of what ought to remain covered, some sexual secret that will be exposed in the universal unveiling of the apocalypse. The ideology causes the social structure of repression and policing, not the other way around, as "The Minister's Black Veil" shows. It does this not least by insisting so dramatically that the black veil is no more than an innocent piece of black cloth. This means that all the "horror" and "terrors" the veil inspires in the people of Milford, including Hooper himself, is a piece of ideological mystification, in spite of the fact that everyone, and Hooper especially, "feel . . . that a preternatural horror was interwoven with the threads of the black crape" (380).

The black veil cannot be lifted because it is not a veil at all, not at least in the sense that a veil implies some secret behind it. The most powerful effect of "The Minister's Black Veil" is to give its readers the chance to escape the ideology associated with the veil by showing an example of that ideology's destructive effects. At the same time the reader can learn that it *is* an ideology, in the specific sense of being produced by confusion between linguistic and material reality. The story is a splendid example of the way a work of literature, if it is read "rhetorically", can function as a powerful unmasking of the ideology of a culture.

But more needs to be said about how the unveiling of the ideology of unveiling works in this story. The spooky power of the minister in his black veil to transgress the border between life and death, to cause the dead and the living to change places, or to blur the distinction between the two so the church bell can be an audible oxymoron and toll simultaneously for a wedding and for a funeral, reappears in an extraordinary passage explaining why Hooper had to give up his habitual walk to the cemetery at sundown: "Others would make it a point of hardihood to throw themselves in his way. The impertinence of the latter class compelled him to give up his customary walk, at sunset, to the burial ground, for when he leaned pensively over the gate, there would always be faces behind the gravestones, peeping at his black veil. A fable went the rounds, that the stare of the dead people drove him thence" (380). Here again is the motif of the dead face that can look, a stare from dead eyes, but it is the living in this case who are turned into the dead. The faces of the living spectators peeping at Hooper from behind the tombstones become the faces of the dead. To look at Hooper in his veil is to be turned into a ghost, a corpse, or into a dead face, the sort of face one sees carved on a tombstone, or the sort of ghost that haunts graveyards.

The sentences just quoted present a miniature allegory of the metonymic relation between an engraved face on a tombstone, for example those winged faces one sees on old New England gravestones, the tombstone itself, the dead body beneath it, the inscription on the tombstone, and the survivor who looks at the tombstone, with its picture and inscription. Each of these but the last, we ordinarily like to think, is a displacement of the others and can stand for it, while the survivor remains safely outside the system. The mere presence of Hooper in his black veil confounds these distinctions. He turns the living spectators into ghosts with dead stares. This exposes the way the whole system of displacements is figurative. We realize that we are ourselves living corpses, spirits imprisoned within a body that will be our tomb, as Socrates long ago said. We readers of "The Minister's Black Veil" may even glimpse for a moment the fact that we are after all reading an inscription, the text of the story, black marks on the pages. We personify this inscription, endow it with a face and voice, and think of the good Mr Hooper as a real person. As readers we raise the dead, and a fictive dead at that, in this twice-told tale that folds the fictive story of Hooper, existing only in Hawthorne's words, over the real tale of the historical Reverend Moody of York, Maine.

The last episode of the story is the final example of the way the wearing of the black veil transgresses the proper distinctions between death and life. On his deathbed the Reverend Hooper refuses the exhortations of the Reverend Clark from Westbury to remove the veil at last, now that he is about to cross the border between life and death, time and eternity. "Are you ready", asks the visitor, "for the lifting of the veil, that shuts in time from eternity?" (383). To remove the veil now will anticipate the apocalyptic unveiling after death Hooper has all along promised.

Hooper refuses to unveil himself. He makes a final speech terrifying his auditors by defining the everyday faces people present to the world as so many more black veils: "I look around me, and, lo! on every visage a Black Veil" (384). Hooper then falls back dead, "a veiled corpse . . . , and a veiled corpse they bore him to the grave" (384). Even beyond death he remains veiled, in defiance of the apocalyptic promise of a postmortal unveiling. The unveiling after death is expressed by the viewing of the face of the corpse in its open coffin or, in earlier European culture, by the visibility of the open face of the tombstone effigy. Instead of that, all of Hooper's parishioners and the readers of his story must think of him as still veiled when he has crossed the border into the realm of death and ought to be unveiled at last.

The promise of an imminent unveiling, it appears, is a promise that can never be kept. However much more time has passed, the unveiling that will make all hearts open to one another and to God through the openness of all faces can never take place. It is always something that is about to happen, just a little bit in the future. Other people may die. We may witness their deaths, as Hooper's parishioners see him fall back "a veiled corpse", but we can never witness our own deaths and subsequent uncovering. We can never experience our own deaths as present events, though those would be the only deaths worth experiencing.

To die and to live through one's death as one's own survivor: which of us has not dreamed of doing that? Anything short of that is of no use, as Hawthorne's story demonstrates. The other person dies, crosses the frontier between life and death. But he or she leaves us with nothing that we can put our hands on as an experience of the promised unveiling. We are left with a mute corpse, an insignificant or non-signifying sign, or a sign that the barrier has not been, for us the survivors, breeched. Hooper dies. He is buried and rots in the ground, still veiled. His remaining veiled is the "type and symbol" of the failure of another's death to give the survivors any experience of the region of death, where all veils are supposed to be removed, all faces open.

The last sentence of the story is therefore perhaps the most unsettling formulation of all in this unsettling tale. It forecloses once and for all the revelation promised by the initial designation of the story as a "parable". We as readers, like the good people of Milford who survive Hooper, are left in exactly the same situation we have always been in. We await an unveiling one displaced name for which is "death": "Good Mr Hooper's face is dust; but awful is still the thought, that it mouldered beneath the Black Veil!" (384).

Just why does the simple act of wearing the black veil cause all this devastation in the little community of Milford? The catastrophic effect seems outrageously incommensurate with its trivial cause. The wearing of the veil, I answer, suspends two of the basic assumptions that make society possible: the assumption that a person's face is the sign of his selfhood and the accompanying presumption that this sign can in one way or another be read. A whole series of presuppositions accompany those assumptions: the presupposition that there are natural as opposed to arbitrary signs, in this case the face; the presupposition that the face as exterior and visible natural sign refers to an interior, non-linguistic entity, the consciousness, subjectivity, soul, or selfhood of the person who presents that face to the world; the presupposition that the procedure whereby we read a person's selfhood by his or her face is paradigmatic for sign-reading in general. The reading of person by face can then be universally extended to the reading of all natural and supernatural entities, all entities not persons – the absent, the inanimate, the dead. This reading would be expressed by those most basic of tropes, prosopopoeia and apostrophe, as in Wordsworth's opening address in "The Boy of Winander": "There was a boy: ye knew him well,

ye cliffs / And islands of Winander!" It is all very well to
say that of course we know that reading a personality by a
face is a precarious dependence on an unreliable trope, but
we go on knowing, choosing, and deciding in daily life as
if this were not the case. Hawthorne's story shows that if
the originary figure of reading self by face is put in question, then the whole set of assumptions making individual
and social life possible are suspended.

When he puts on the black veil the Reverend Hooper is
as if he were already dead. Or, rather, he seems already to
have withdrawn to that realm where signs cannot reach,
for which "death" is one name. Or, rather, it is as if the
simple act of putting on the black veil had revealed the
unverifiable possibility that each of us already dwells in
that realm, both as we are for other people and even as we
are for ourselves. The black veil reveals in these effects
the possibility that unveiling, apocalyptic or otherwise, is
impossible.

The most literal and direct effect of the veil is to suspend
for Hooper's parishioners access to his subjectivity. His
"figure" becomes ambiguous, disquietingly attractive, fascinating, just because his face has become invisible. This
is expressed by a regular distinction between "face" and
"figure" that Hawthorne borrows from common parlance:
"Strangers came long distances to attend services at his
church, with the mere idle purpose of gazing at his figure,
because it was forbidden them to behold his face" (381).

Hooper's last words, "I look around me, and, lo! on
every visage a Black Veil" (384), assert that the face itself
is a veil. Hooper's corpse mouldering in the earth, still
veiled, is a veiled veil, a veil on top of a veil. There is no
reason to assume that even the most extravagant series of
unveilings would ever reach anything but another veil.
Death, as Paul de Man says, is "a displaced name for a
linguistic predicament".[15] This is the predicament of never
being able to name the realities we most want to name –
the self, nature, God, the realm beyond the borders of life

– except in that unverifiable trope called a catachresis. Catachresis often takes the form of a prosopopoeia, as in "face of a mountain" or "eye of a storm". Such a trope defaces or disfigures in the very act whereby it ascribes a face to what has none.

Hawthorne gives striking typological expression to this predicament in his image of the veiled face as a veil behind a veil. The black veil is literally a de-facement or disfigurement. It deprives Hooper of the face whereby his neighbours assume they know him. However one wishes to describe it generically, as allegorical personification, or as parabolic realism, or as apocalyptic prophecy, the veil as type or symbol de-faces that for which it stands. At the same time the veil disfigures its referent in another way. The veil between us and that for which it is a type and a symbol is an enigmatic sign that appears to give access to what it stands for while forbidding the one who confronts it to move behind it by any effort of hermeneutic interpretation. If Hooper's face behind the veil, like that of all his neighbours, is yet another veil, then it can be said that the real face too is not a valid sign but another de-facement. The face de-faces . . . it.

Systematic narrative and figurative notations in the story of the things that are covered by a black veil extend the meaning of veiling to cover the whole repertoire of those entities that are the outside grounding of social life: nature, God, death, or the realm we shall enter after death. It is as if the inaccessibility of what the black veil covers makes it spread out to include not just Hooper's face as the sign of his selfhood but the whole array of things that are the threatening exterior of social life, while at the same time presumed to be its secure foundation.

When Hooper's subjectivity becomes inaccessible by way of his face, his veil covers a kind of floating location of the unlocatable. The spectator's speculations about what may be behind the veil drifts from consciousness to the place of death, to God, to nature. Hawthorne's story implicitly recognizes that prosopopoeia is the primary means by which mankind names and tames all that is outside the human. We give nature, God, or death a human face in order to give ourselves the illusion that we can have access to them, understand them, appropriate them as the grounds of our social intercourse. But Hooper's wearing the black veil, by suspending that primary "literal" prosopopoeia whereby we interpret a person's facial features as the signs of his or her selfhood, suspends also those extensions of prosopopoeia that are ordinarily so taken for granted as not even to be recognizable as tropes, for example when we call nature "she".

When Hooper is affrighted by his own face in the mirror during the wedding service, he rushes forth into the darkness: "For the Earth, too, had on her Black Veil." "Dying sinners" shudder when Hooper puts his veiled face near their own, "such were the terrors of the black veil, even when Death had bared his visage" (381). In his deathbed speech Hooper speaks of the way man now does "vainly shrink from the eye of his Creator" (384). All these prosopopoeias – Earth as a woman, Death as man, God as possessing an all-seeing eye – discreetly signalled by capitals, by pronouns, or by the projection on what is not human of parts of the human body, are so inextricably woven into everyday speech as to be almost invisible. They are almost effaced or "dead" metaphors. Of course we speak of the earth as "she". Of course we speak of being face to face with death, or of being under the eye of God. How could we speak at all of these things otherwise? Such universal tropes become visible only when they are suspended. Prosopopoeia is essential to allegory, as in the capitalizations of Earth, Death, and Creator here. How could there be allegory without abstractions personified and capitalized, "Orgoglio" in Spenser, or "Caritas" and the rest in Giotto's Allegory of the Virtues and Vices at Padua? Prosopopoeia is the catachrestic trope that covers our ignor-

ance of nature, death, and God. Prosopopoeia makes everything we say of these, like what we say of the human heart,
an allegory. They are allegorical in the sense of being
simultaneously an unveiling (speaking of Mother Earth
opens up the possibility of incorporating nature into our
discourse), and a veiling (speaking of Mother Earth covers
over the otherness of nature by ascribing to it a spurious
similarity to ourselves).

Much is at stake in being able to go on seeing these
effaced prosopopoeias as valid. At stake is our ability to go
on living with a modest sense of security as mortals in an
alien and threatening universe. At stake also is even our
sense of ourselves *as* selves, since to question those ubiqui-
tous personifications of nature, God, and death is, by a
reciprocal putting in question, to suspend that "literal"
prosopopoeia whereby a human face, our own or that of
another, is an index to a self behind the face. It is no
wonder the good citizens of Milford are appalled.

Hooper performs all this putting-in-question not by a
disarticulating process using language against language.
Such an effort always fails by smuggling back into the
effort of disarticulation the very thing that is being disar-
ticulated, as in my almost effaced prosopopoeia in "smuggling". Hooper's act works because it is done in perhaps
the only way such an act can be effectively perfomed: in a
silent "gesture" that is not really a gesture, since it is not
part of a usual system of bodily movements, and by the
proffering of a sign that is not really a sign, since its referent
and its signification remain forever unverifiable. He appears
wearing a black veil.

The performative effect of this silent act can be compared
to the equally devastating effect of Bartleby's "I would
prefer not to," in Melville's "Bartleby the Scrivener".[16] In
both cases, once by an act of language, once by an act
outside of language, language is brought to a stop, rendered
powerless. This inhibition includes all kinds of language:
narrative language, language conceptual, dialectical, criti-

cal, historical, biographical, and so on. In the "The Minister's Black Veil" it can be said that the efforts of Hooper's parishioners, of Hooper himself, of the narrator of his story, of Hawthorne, and of all readings of the story, including this one, are unavailing attempts to find language adequate to reincorporate into our everyday world the mute sign Hooper displays as an affront to his community.

It is now possible to answer the question, "Of what, then, is The 'Minister's Black Veil' a parable?" The story is not simply a parable of the working of parable, as opposed to being the parabolic expression of a "spiritual" meaning, a meaning capable of being expressed in no other way. Biblical scholars and critics of secular parables, such as those of Kafka, have observed that all parables tend to be about their own working. Jesus's parable of the sower is the paradigmatic example. This would not be enough to say about "The Minister's Black Veil". Of this story it would be better to say that it is the indirect, veiled expression of the impossibility of expressing anything verifiable at all in parable except the impossibility of expressing anything verifiable.

The veil is the type and symbol of the fact that all signs are potentially unreadable, or that the reading of them is potentially unverifiable. If the reader has no access to what lies behind a sign but another sign, then all reading of signs cannot be sure whether or not it is in error. Reading would then be a perpetual wandering or displacement that can never be checked against anything except another sign. If the artwork should be, in Kant's formulation, the indispensable bridge between epistemology and ethics, from knowledge to justified action, Hawthorne's story, it can be said, puts all its readers together on that bridge, stuck there without entrance or egress, able to go neither forward nor backward, neither back to certain knowledge of what the story means nor forward to conscientious ethical or political action in the real world.

This situation is intolerable. To live is to act, to need to act, and to need to act with a sense that we are justified in what we do. We would do anything to escape from this situation or to persuade ourselves that we are not in it. "The Minister's Black Veil" presents the reader with a full repertoire of the ways this attempt can be made. All critical essays on the story are so many more attempts to put something verifiable behind the veil, to make the veil the type and symbol of something definite one can confront directly, face to face, *through* the veil, by means of the veil. Each of these attempts proffers an hypothesis about the meaning of the veil. Each proposes or posits some entity there. This is followed, in each case, by unsuccessful attempts to verify this hypothesis, or by an implicit recognition in the act of positing the hypothesis that it is intrinsically unverifiable.

I have already cited passages in which Hooper's parishioners imagine that some stranger may have changed places with their pastor. I have also cited the discussion with Elizabeth in which Hooper answers the direct request to "take away the veil" if not from his face then from the enigmatic or "mysterious" words he uses to explain the veil. He answers only in terms of riddling "ifs": "Know, then, this veil is a type and a symbol . . . *If* it be a sign of mourning . . . *If* I hide my face for sorrow . . . and *if* I cover it for secret sin" (378–379, my italics). But Elizabeth, Hooper's parishioners, the narrator, Hooper himself, and the reader do not want "ifs" and "perhapses". We want certainty. In response to that hermeneutic need the good citizens of Milford suppose there must be some specific cause or explanation for Hooper's taking the veil. They conclude, for example, from the fact that he avoids looking at his own veiled face that, like the Reverend Moody of York, though by intent rather than by accident, he must have performed some deeply guilty act: "This was what gave plausibility to the whispers, that Mr Hooper's conscience tortured him for some great crime, too horrible to be entirely concealed, or otherwise than so obscurely intimated" (380). On the other hand, according to another hypothesis, they suppose that Hooper must be possessed and may be consorting with the devil behind the veil: "It was said, that ghost or fiend consorted with him there" (380). Another possibility, proposed to herself earlier by Elizabeth, is that the wearing of the veil "was perhaps a symptom of mental disease" (379). The operative words here are *perhaps*, *obscurely*, and *or*. It may be this or it may be that. There is no way to tell. Whatever hypothesis anyone makes about what is behind the veil, whatever proposal, proposition, or positing anyone makes, remains just that, an unverifiable hypothesis. There is no way, in this life, once you have accepted the complex ideology of the veil, to get behind the veil to find out what is really going on back there, though this is what that ideology leads us to want to do.

If, after death, good Mr Hooper's face "mouldered beneath the Black Veil," this suggests the inextricable involvement of the inaccessibility of death in the ideological system of veiling. It confirms that death is indeed a displaced name for a linguistic predicament, the predicament of being able to posit or project names freely, in primal personifying apostrophes, but unable to validate those names by any direct experience of what is named. The positing itself erects a barrier or veil. Such naming is premimetic or pre-representational, that is, it does not point toward anything that can be directly experienced. At the same time such naming forbids ever entering a representational or mimetic domain where words can be matched with things known directly, prior to language. The face is a defacing, as the *pro* ("in front of, before") in *prosopon* or *prosopopoeia* suggests. *Prosopon* means face *or* mask, the face as mask put in front of an unfathomable enigma. The figure of the face as that which is "in front" of something behind is present still in all our English words in "front": "confront", "affront", "frontal", and "front" itself. These come from Latin *frons*: "forehead", "brow". The title of Hardy's "In Front of the Landscape", for example, is already a covert prosopopoeia, as is a colloquial phrase like "the front of the house". The most disquieting effect of Hooper's veil, as the story makes clear in Hooper's last speech, is to show that the face itself is already an impenetrable veil. A veiled face is a veil over a veil, a veiling of what is already veiled.

Even for Hooper, who lives behind the veil and should therefore know what it typifies, the sight of his veiled face is terrifying. This is the case not because the veil signifies a secret guilt of which he is aware, nor because he knows that he consorts with the devil behind it — no textual support is given to these hypotheses — but because for him too its meaning cannot be specified and then verified. Though he is behind the veil, when he catches a glimpse of his veiled face in the mirror he is as much outside the veil as anyone else. For Hooper too the meaning of the veil is a matter of "if", of "perhaps", and of the "or" of ambiguity.

Nor is Hooper himself exempt from the irresistible temptation to make the veil typify something definite in order to escape from the unbearable suspension of not knowing for sure. His proposal involves speculations not about what is within his own hidden subjectivity, except insofar as it is hidden even from himself, but rather speculations about what is beyond the grave, beyond even that apocalyptic unveiling when all shall be revealed: "What, but the mystery which it obscurely typifies, has made this piece of crape so awful? When the friend shows his inmost heart to his friend; the lover to his best-beloved; when man does not vainly shrink from the eye of his Creator, loathsomely treasuring up the secret of his sin; then deem me a monster, for the symbol beneath which I have lived, and die!" (384).

The black veil is the presentation not so much of a secular symbol as of a spiritual symbol that has only an individual authority, just as, within Protestantism gener-

ally, or New England Puritanism in particular, every man
may be his own priest, his own validation for a testimony
that goes beyond biblical precedent and institutional authority. The minister's veil extrapolates beyond the biblical
texts about veils, just as Hawthorne's story is a parable
added in supplement to the canonical parables of Jesus in
the New Testament. As I began my discussion of the story
by saying, Hooper nowhere claims that his authority for
wearing the veil is some special mission, election, or calling
that has commanded him to do so as witness to some
peculiar insight mediated to his congregation by means of
the veil. He is conspicuously silent where he might speak
out, by saying "God commanded me to do it", or "A still
small voice told me to do it", or even, "The devil made
me do it". He just does it. Though Hooper becomes an
awesome power in the New England church, a famous
preacher who strikes religious terror into the hearts of all
who hear him, that church dispatches a representative to
his deathbed to try (unsuccessfully) to persuade Hooper to
remove the veil before he dies. His stubborn refusal is seen
as a scandal by his church.

Moreover, the traditional theological terminology of
Hooper's refusal (in the words "mystery" and "obscurely
typifies") is displaced to name the linguistic predicament I
have identified. The emphasis is on that particular form of
this predicament so fascinating to Hawthorne: the incommensurability of solitary consciousness and any language
whatsoever that "may be understood and felt by anybody,
who will give himself the trouble to read it" (Preface to
Twice-told Tales, 1152). The logic of Hooper's formulation
turns on "when" and "then". *When* each of us does not
hide his inmost heart from God, from those closest to him,
even from himself, or as Hooper has put it in his initial
sermon after he dons the Black Veil, when we no longer
cover "those sad mysteries which we hide from our nearest
and dearest, and would fain conceal from our own consciousness, even forgetting that the Omniscient can detect

them" (373), *then* "deem me a monster, for the symbol beneath which I have lived, and die!" The now of that "then", however, has not yet come. In this life it remains the imminence of a perpetual "not quite yet" within which "every visage" is a Black Veil, as impenetrable as Hooper's literal veil of crape. Within the time of waiting for that perpetually deferred uncovering, Hooper is not a monster, or not yet a monster, unless all others are monsters too, though it *would* be monstrous to wear the black veil still, after the universal unveiling at the apocalypse.

Monster: the word means "showing forth", the demonstration of something hideously unlawful or unique, for example, a monstrous birth. Now Hooper is not a monster because all men and women are monsters. All manifest, in spite of themselves, the sign of the nameless and unattainable secrets all hide in their hearts, secrets monstrously different in each case. The singularity of selfhood, its uniqueness, the impossibility of fitting selfhood into any categories of genre or species, and the impossibility of saying anything definite about it are, as I have said, perhaps that "Unpardonable Sin" Ethan Brand seeks everywhere in the world and then finds in his own heart. The unpardonable sin is that sin beyond the reach of language, beyond even that particular form of performative language called a pardon, beyond even God's speech of pardon, if not beyond God's all-seeing eye. How awful to be visible to God but beyond the reach of God's pardoning word!

Hooper dies not only still veiled, but still with "a faint smile lingering on the lips" (384). This dimly glimmering smile is the sign of his characteristic irony, meaning by irony a perpetual suspension of definite meaning. Hooper's smile accompanies the unresolvable ambiguity of the veil itself and of everything that is said about it, by the narrator, by the people of Milford, and by Hooper himself, however desperate all of these are to put an end to that ambiguity by saying something definite and verifiable about the meaning of the veil. Hooper's neighbours, the narrator, and the readers of the story are driven to extravagant unverifiable hypotheses by the juxtaposition of that faint smile and the surmounting blank black veil, marked only by its fold. I suggested earlier that the fold in the veil may perhaps be related to the twice-telling of this tale and to the way a secondary parabolic meaning is superimposed on the primary literal meaning. It would be just as plausible to relate the folding to the double meaning of irony. The two signs, the dim smile without a face and the folded veil above it, would then mean the same thing or would double one another. They would be the type and symbol of the radical undecidability of all ironic expression, even of that form of ironic expression that is not verbal but facial. Irony keeps its own counsel. It responds to our interrogations only with a further ironic smile or with an ominously permissive, "Of course, if you say so".

Insofar as Hooper's sin is the sin of irony, it is appropriate that the story should end with his death, since death and irony have a secret and unsettling alliance. Though Hooper, unlike Socrates, is not put to death for being an ironist, in both cases irony is shown to be lethal. It is deadly both for the ironist and for those on whom the irony is inflicted. Irony puts both the ironist and his victims in proximity to death, but it ironically survives the death of the ironist to go on through perhaps centuries of human history effecting its deadly work of the suspension of that definite meaning for which we all long and which we all think we ought to have. The putting to death of Socrates did not put an end to the effect of Socrates's irony, as the citizens of Athens may have hoped. Quite the contrary, as any good reader of the Platonic dialogues knows. And the citizens of Milford, like the narrator, who in his last sentence places the events he has been telling at a firm historical distance ("The grass of many years has sprung up and withered on that grave" [394]), are still haunted by the memory of Hooper's smile and by the image of his face mouldering beneath the veil.

*

The attempt by the characters and by the narrator to put an end to painful hermeneutic suspension is continued by all the commentaries on Hawthorne's story that propose some definite explanation of it. One example would be an explanation in terms of history: "The Minister's Black Veil" is a representation by Hawthorne of the historical situation of New England Puritanism surviving into a Franklinian society. Another explanation would appeal to the psychology of the author: "The Minister's Black Veil" expresses Hawthorne's obsession with the theme of secret sin or guilt. Another explanation would be based on inter-textual analogies: "The Minister's Black Veil" is to be read in terms of its echoes of similar themes and figures in other works by Hawthorne, for example the motif of the veil in *The Blithedale Romance* and *The Marble Faun*, or the motif of secret sexual transgression in *The Scarlet Letter*, or the theme of unpardonable sin in "Ethan Brand". D. A. Miller's Foucauldian interpretation of the story, discussed above, argues that the story is made definite in meaning when it is placed in the context of nineteenth-century ideas about sexual secrets. My reading differs in principle from all these in being an unveiling and putting in question of the ideology of unveiling that inveigles Hooper, his community, and most readers of the story into believing that there must be something definite behind the veil – both Hooper's veil and the veil of the text as the words on the page – and that our business as readers is to identify it.

"The Minister's Black Veil", both the veil itself, *in* the story, and the text of the story in the sense of the materiality of the letter, the words there on the page, patiently endures all these positings and projections of meaning, but it does not unequivocally endorse any of them. It offers itself to be read. If there is a veil in the text that all those inside the story want desperately to pierce or to lift so they can name once and for all what is behind it, for readers of

"The Minister's Black Veil", here and now in 1990, the text itself is a veil we would pierce or lift. This desire to establish a definitive meaning for the black veil by relating it to something behind it for which it stands is an example of the hermeneutic desire as such. This desire would put a stop to the endless drifting of interpretation by saying, once and for all, "The veil means so and so". The reader shares this desire with Hooper's congregation, with his fiancée, with Hooper himself. This might be expressed by saying that the story is an allegory of the reader's own situation in reading it. If this hermeneutic desire could be appeased, then example could be a confirmation of theory, or a means of adjusting it so it could be confirmed. Allegory and realism would then be reconciled, since the realistic story would be the unambiguous carrier of a definite allegorical meaning. Language and history would be brought to touch one another, merge, overlap.

This happy reconciliation, this crossing over by means of parable into the land of parable, behind the veil, does not in this case occur. One remembers Lewis Carroll's poem of "The Walrus and the Carpenter". To the final interrogation of the oysters, "answer came there none, / Which was not surprising since / They'd eaten every one." Of all our interrogations of the veil of "The Minister's Black Veil", as of the interrogations of the veil itself within the story, it can be said "answer came there none". This is not because the text is a self-consuming artifact that eats itself up through some internal contradiction or undecidability. Rather, the attempt to turn the opacity of parabolic symbol into transparent concept is the eating up of the text. The text says what it says, if it says anything, in the way parable does, that is, by way of opaque symbols that resist translation into perspicuous concepts. To say of the veil it is a symbol of sin, it is sorrow, it is madness, it is New England Puritanism in a Franklinian culture, or it is the cover for sexual secrets is to receive no response from the text.

The text remains silent. It gives no answer to our questions, though it endures being translated into the unverifiable concepts which eat it up. Such translations make the story disappear from the page and become those blank pages in the sunlight Hawthorne feared all his works were. To alter the metaphor again: "The Minister's Black Veil", like Bartleby in Melville's story, answers to all our demands: "I should prefer not to." Like Bartleby's phrase, with its conditional "should", its gently indecisive "prefer", both inhibiting the "not" from being the negative of some positive and thereby something we can make part of some dialectical reasoning, "The Minister's Black Veil" is neither positive nor negative. It is patiently neutral. It says neither yes nor no to whatever hypotheses about it the reader proposes. The text offers neither confirmation nor disconfirmation of any speculative formulation about its meaning.

In this the text is like the black veil itself. The performative efficacy of "The Minister's Black Veil" lies in this similarity. It works. Like the veil, the story is a strange kind of efficacious speech act. It is a way of doing things with proffered signs. But it does to undo, to take away foundation or authority from anything any reader can say of it.

To speak of performative efficacy is to return, finally, to the last element in the sequence with which I began. That sequence went from Theory to Example to Reading to History. Any speech act is historical. It takes place at a certain place and time. To say "takes place" is to be reminded both of the oddness of that idiom and of the oddness of speech acts, which "take place", occupy space-time, in acts which are no more violent than the uttering of an "I do" or the signing of one's name. Nevertheless, they may be followed by, and appear to authorize, events of the utmost physical violence: revolutions, wars, deportations, executions. A speech act is a way in which language may enter into history by "making something happen" in the solid world of flesh and blood people and of material and economic facts.

But it will not do to take "history" for granted as something manifest, as plain as the nose on your face. "History" is not necessarily something we already know and understand. Nor can we assume that the line from speech act to material historical event is to be understood on the model of causal determination.[17] "History", as a term and as a "thing", is as problematic, as much a question rather than an answer, as "matter", "nature", "experience", "self-hood", or any of the other concepts or entities we might wish to take for granted as solid starting places – so we can get on with the serious work of the human sciences.

The question of the relation between literature and history is a frontier area for thinking about interpretation in the humanities these days. It would seem that what is sometimes called "the linguistic turn" in the human sciences has taken place, once and for all. John E. Toews defines this paradigm shift in a challenging and wide-ranging review essay. After having agreed with William J. Bowsma that the "focus on the production, reproduction, and transmission of meanings in various historical periods and cultural contexts [is at] the center of the most interesting and innovative work being produced, not only by . . . historians but more generally in the humanities and social sciences", Toews goes on to define the linguistic turn as follows: "Most seem ready to concede that language can no longer be construed as simply a medium, relatively or potentially transparent, for the representation or expression of a reality outside of itself and are willing to entertain seriously some form of semiological theory in which language is conceived of as a self-contained system of 'signs' whose meanings are determined by their relations to each other, rather than by their relations to some 'transcendental' or extralinguistic object or subject." One basic presupposition of "the new, semiologically oriented history of meanings" is "the assumption that meanings do not mirror or represent but actually constitute or create the reality experienced by human beings". Another is the assumption that "both text and context are complex relations of signifying practices", from which it follows that "the context never 'explains' the text in the sense of providing the essence of its appearance or the cause of its effect or the reality of its representation."[18]

I would almost completely agree with Toews's description of the "linguistic turn". I say "almost" because there seems to me some remnant of the duality being contested in saying that "meanings" "constitute or create" "the reality experienced by human beings". In this formulation "meanings" are still opposed to "experience", even though the former are said to "constitute" the latter. I should say, on the contrary, that the "linguistic turn" means seeing experience as permeated through and through by signs, indistinguishable from them. Moreover, I should put "rhetorical" in pace of Toews's word "semiological". To say "rhetorical theory" rather than "semiological theory" would recognize the way the linguistic turn affirms the role of figurative language in the "constitution of meanings" and the way it grants a performative as well as a constative or cognitive dimension to language. Nevertheless, I am glad to learn that the linguistic turn is beginning to have such force now within the discipline of history proper. I make two presuppositions, however, about this "turn". First: the shift to the view Toews describes is not as easy to make as he seems to assume. Stubborn traces of the older assumption that history is something solidly out there, external to language or to other sign-systems, remain in the formulations even of those who think themselves fully committed to the new view. An example is some of the work of the so-called "new historicists" in literary study, in spite of their great methodological sophistication. Second: the most important methodological problem in humanistic studies now is to refine our understanding of the particular form of sign to sign connection involved in the relation of text to context, for example the relation of a work of literature to history. What I shall say here about Hawthorne's "The Minister's Black Veil" is meant as a start toward that refinement.

History enters or is entered into a number of different points by "The Minister's Black Veil". Hawthorne's writing of the story was a historical event. It occurred at a specific place and time in history. It was itself a response to a historical event or condition: New England Puritanism as it existed in the past and was still a force in Hawthorne's own time. But "The Minister's Black Veil" was not so much caused by those antecedent historical events as it was a reading of them. Or, since any conceivable traces, remnants, records, or memorials of New England Puritanism, were already a reading, it would be better to say that Hawthorne's story was a re-reading of history, with all the connotations of violence involved in the concept of appropriative reading-again. In Hawthorne's story history is turned into a parable presented in the form of a memorial record of a pseudo-historical event. However paradigmatic of New England Puritanism the Reverend Hooper of Milford may be, he never existed as such in history. He is a fictional historical personage. Such imaginary personages may have great historical force, as may real historical personages when fictionalized in our memory.

"The Minister's Black Veil" was first published in 1836, in *The Token*, then republished in 1837 in the first collection of *Twice-told Tales*. The latter was underwritten without Hawthorne's knowledge or consent by Horatio Bridge. The story was published again in 1851 and then on down through the years in a multitude of editions and anthologies. All these printings were historical occurrences of the most concrete and material sort. They are embedded in the social and economic history, as well as the intellectual history, of the United States. But the metaphor in "embedded" is as problematic and question-begging as are any of the other metaphors by which we try to speak of the relation of a literary text to history. Is the text "embedded" in history, as my formulation suggests, or is history "embedded" in the text, as Stephen Greenblatt's way of putting it affirms?

Each reading of "The Minister's Black Veil", finally, is another historical event. Salient examples are Poe's reading, discussed above, or Melville's reading as recorded incidentally in his review essay "Hawthorne and His Mosses": "I have thus far omitted all mention of his 'Twice-Told Tales', and 'Scarlet Letter'. Both are excellent; but full of such manifold, strange and diffusive beauties, that time would all but fail me, to point the half of them out."[19] Other examples would include Henry James's reading, as recorded in his book on Hawthorne, cited at the beginning of this essay, and my present reading, here and now, along with all those other articles on the story I have cited in my bibliographical footnote.

All these moments, at the beginning, along the way, and at "the end", when the story was written, published, and whenever the story is read, are so many historical events. They are moments when language enters life. How can we define what happens in those moments, as exactly as possible?

The story told in "The Minister's Black Veil" provides an answer, if we choose to take it as such. The story offers the reader a model, a paradigm or parabolic expression, of what a historical event is. On the other hand, the story itself, as a physical object, black marks on paper, a man-made object produced at certain times and places, is also in its writing, publication, and reading a series of historical events of the most literal and material kind. The story told within the text is analogous to the performative working of the text thought of as a physical event. In this "The Minister's Black Veil", as its subtitle affirms, is a parable. Like the parables of Jesus it is about what it does, though Hawthorne's story is a written or printed speech act rather than an oral performance. Nor does it claim divine authority. Moreover, Jesus's telling of one of his parables happened one unique time, whereas Hawthorne's written and then printed parable makes something happen whenever and wherever it is read. It does this on occasions that are always to some degree different from one another. But who could deny that *readings* of the parables of Jesus, as they were recorded by the Gospel writers, have not had historical effects?

Parable in "The Minister's Black Veil" is folded over itself. To put this another way, what the story makes happen has two temporal vectors, one facing toward the past, the other toward the future. Both vectors are present at any point in the text. On the one hand, "The Minister's Black Veil" is explicitly presented, by way of its initial footnote, as a re-reading or re-writing of a past event – re-writing as re-reading. That either, both, or neither of these events is fictitious does not affect the story's parabolic power. Or does it? What difference does it make whether a parable uses real history or pretended history as its analogical base? Does not parable break down that distinction by showing historical events to be always already parabolic? In any case, Hawthorne's story is a twice-telling with a difference of the story of the Reverend Moody, whose wearing of the veil "had a different import". It is not necessary for Hooper to know that he is repeating Moody in a different mode for what he does to function as a repetition. It might even be the case that a parabolic happening requires, as an essential requisite for its working, the forgetting of the antecedents it repeats.

If "The Minister's Black Veil" is a valid example, it would seem that historical events are not so much the conscious repetition of earlier historical events as their inadvertent re-enactment. This re-enactment works on its own. It is not dependent on the conscious intention of the new actors on the stage of history. The new event functions as a re-reading, perhaps as a misreading and distortion, of previous events. This happens even if the characters performing the repetition are not aware that they are doing again something already done. Marx, in a notorious passage in "The Eighteenth Brumaire", asserts that a historical event occurs twice, once as tragedy and then again as farce. His example is the repetition of Napoleon Bonaparte by Louis Napoleon. But the French Revolution and its culmination in Napoleon's conquests was itself already, in this case self-consciously, the repetition of Roman history. What may not have been known was the farcical quality of this repetition.

The second definition of an historical event, still taking "The Minister's Black Veil" as a paradigm, is that it is the irruption of a sign or system of signs into the historical continuum. This entrance is oriented toward the future. The new sign is the differential repetition of an earlier sign. Good Mr Hooper appears wearing his black veil. This manifestation or monstration breaks into Milford's communal life. Milford is never the same again. Hawthorne writes and publishes "The Minister's Black Veil". American history is, in however small a degree, never quite the same. Our history is once more disrupted, always in unpredictable ways, every time the story is read. This feature of unannounced breaking in is essential to historical happenings, as Walter Benjamin asserts in his "Theses on the Philosophy of History".

Hooper's appearance in the black veil, Hawthorne's writing and publication of "The Minister's Black Veil", any reading of the story, are not parables of what an historical event is. They are literal historical happenings, whether real or fictive. If this is so, an historical happening is not what it is sometimes still thought to be, in spite of that so-called linguistic turn. We are still likely to think of history as in one way or another something solidly extra-textual. History, we think, must be a physical or material occurrence that happens outside language, like an earthquake or the explosion of a star. History must therefore be knowable by consciousness and namable in straightforward referential language. But "The Minister's Black Veil" suggests that a historical event cannot be fully incorporated into concepts of exteriority, material fact, "experience", the body, power, force, social or economic "realities".

Nevertheless, some such conception of history is often invoked these days as the rock of reality, the ultimate point of reference in the human sciences or in cultural studies, including literary criticism. A return to the materiality of history is sometimes invoked as an antidote to language-oriented theory, a return to reality from the disembodied speculations of theorists who see everything as language, the world as text, and language as the endless "play" of signs in the void. It is easy to understand the rage of those who want to get back from language to reality, to history, to facts, to the material world. We want, as Marx said in his rejection of Hegel, to pass from language to life. But if "The Minister's Black Veil" has any paradigmatic validity, a historical event is not to be understood as representation, nor as memory, nor as the direct experience in the present of events that take place before some spectator's eyes. If history were any of these things, it could then be written down in a memorial record to be later re-read by future generations of historians. This reading would provide access to "history as it really happened" or at any rate to the subjective responses of those before whose eyes history really happned.

A historical happening, "The Minister's Black Veil" suggests, is not a factual event out there in the world perceived by some witness or experienced by some participant in a way that can be accounted for by some version of a subject to object or subject to subject relation. Nor can a historical event be "represented", more or less accurately, in language. Nor does history remain safely stored up in traces, texts, memorials, records, vestiges, or material artifacts that can then later on be deciphered by future generations as the means of access to the original happening as it really happened. Nor are we justified in thinking of history as a purely physical occurrence, like an earthquake or the appearance of a nova in the sky. Insofar as such contingent cataclysms are historical happenings, they too occur in the same way that the minister's appearance in the veil or the publication of "The Minister's Black Veil" happens.

What then is that way of historical happening, if it is not to be thought of in any of those ways we are likely spontaneously to think it can be thought? We do this under the command of powerful ideological presuppositions, assumptions difficult to see for what they are, rather than just as "common sense". If I take "The Minister's Black Veil" as a parable of history, I must say that a historical happening is not representable but performative. A historical event is a speech act of a particular kind, the kind that involves the putting forth and then the reading of a sign. The exploding star and the earthquake are in this no different from the story. What is true of all three is true of historical events in general. The star and the earthquake too are signs, in the heavens, on the earth. They are signs that have a material embodiment, like all signs. They become history when those signs are read. The explosion of the star in the Large Magellanic Cloud, the earthquake in Lisbon, in Chile, or in California, come to exist as historical events through the reading of all the data received from the star or in the reading of the meaning of the earthquake by some witness – that it was God's vengeance or that it was the product of great forces to be explained by plate tectonics.

In the case of the minister's black veil and "The Minister's Black Veil", as my reading has attempted to demonstrate, the veil and the story are undecidable in meaning. They may mean this or they may mean that. It is impossible to tell for sure which reading is the correct one. I have formulated this as the unveiling of the possibility of the impossibility of unveiling. Though both the veil itself and the story about it contain clues about how they should be read, those clues – the folding of the veil, its blackness, various readings of the veil within the text of the story – do not authorize a single unambiguous reading. The tale mutely submits to whatever reading we impose on it, but it does not unequivocally justify any one reading. In this it is like any "real" historical event. It *is* a real historical event.

Something happens when anyone reads "The Minister's Black Veil". Something certainly happens in the community of Milford when Hooper appears in his veil. But what happens in either case is unpredictable. The effect is incommensurate with its cause. What happens is not "caused" according to some model of physical causality. It depends on how the proffered sign is read, and the sign does not authorize any single reading. If an historical happening is neither a representation nor in itself representable, neither is it a cause nor a result in the ordinary senses of these terms. It is not an element in a complex involving a measurable correspondence between cause and effect.

Let me try, with the help of "The Minister's Black Veil", to explain just how what I have been saying is the case. The story presents a salient example of the way a speech act cannot be assimilated to the logic of cause and effect, since it always involves an act of reading. The Reverend Hooper, the reader is told, became something of a celebrity in New England: "Strangers came long distances to attend service at his church, with the mere idle purpose of gazing at his figure, because it was forbidden to behold his face. But many were made to quake ere they departed!" (381). Hooper, as the years go by, is to a certain extent normalized, assimilated into the community. He becomes one of its regular fixtures, something to take in on a sightseeing trip, like other natural and man-made wonders.

In one case, however, Hooper's preaching has a more serious social effect than scaring those who have come for idle detached looking: "Once, during Governor Belcher's administration, Mr Hooper was appointed to preach the election sermon. Covered with his black veil, he stood before the chief magistrate, the council, the representatives, and wrought so deep an impression, that the legislative measures of that year, were characterized by all the gloom and piety of our earliest ancestral sway" (381). The reader is not told that the sermon recommended specific legislation. Presumably it was his usual sermon about secret sin, the sin we would hide not only from our neighbour, but from ourselves and from God. The chief magistrate, the council, and the representatives, however, take the sermon as the command to enact specific laws, laws characterized by gloom and piety. The sermon is an efficacious speech act. But what it makes happen is not commensurate with its "cause", nor predictable from that cause. The effect of Hooper's sermon goes by way of an act of reading in which the listeners draw their own conclusions. They decide that they should enact certain specific laws, though the narrator does not tell us that Hooper's sermon made any such recommendation. In fact, the narrator emphasizes more the effect of the veil than the sermon in making "so deep an impression". The harsh legislative measures seem to have been caused by the veil. Or, rather, they are the result of an unauthorized reading of the veil. They are one more example of the effect on the community of that simple piece of double-folded black crape.

The black veil and the text of the story are differentiated within themselves, discrepant. They therefore do not give solid grounding to the acts reading them generates. In both cases, however, something does occur, for example the response of the people of Milford to Hooper's appearance in the veil or this present reading of Hawthorne's story. I did not foresee the exact trajectory my essay would take when I sat down to write, any more than I can foresee the effects it will have when it is read aloud or printed, thereby entering history in its turn. Of the story itself and of any conceivable reading of it, one can say what Hawthorne's narrator says of the veil: "Thus, from beneath the black veil, there rolled a cloud into the sunshine, an ambiguity of sin and sorrow . . ." (380).

There is even more to be said, however, still assuming that it is valid to take "The Minister's Black Veil" as a parable of history. The story links the black veil with death and with the mortality of the living. It also presents itself as repetition. The donning of the veil is one link in a chain of similar events that has at least two links, Moody and Hooper – more links if all the shadowily present biblical and literary antecedents are included. This joining of death and repetition indicates that a historical event takes place within a space of time divided within itself by its relation to death. Each historical happening is part of an indefinite series of repetitions stretching before and after.

The veil stands for death, but "death" in this case too is a displaced name for a linguistic predicament. This "predicament" is the impossibility of reaching death through the signs for it. The material base, in this case that black piece of crape, is incommensurate with the parabolic meaning it carries. Each destroys the other or is destroyed by it, leaving the reader with a blank page in the sunlight. A historical happening is both finite and without ascertainable origin or end. The veil or the story about the veil can promise the revelation that is to come, when all veils will be removed, but it cannot escape from the paradox of all apocalyptic texts. The apocalyptic promise is in this world always not quite yet fulfilled. No mortal can experience his or her own death or what preceded his or her coming into the world. To be mortal is, paradoxically, to have no ascertainable beginning or end. A historical event is therefore both finite and at the same time unbounded. It is without borders that may be experienced. This is so because history is something that happens to mortals, that is, to beings whose lives are essentially defined by the fact that they once were not yet and will all one day no longer be. To be mortal is to be surrounded by what lies beyond the limits of experience.

"The Minister's Black Veil" provides a powerful parabolic expression of this. "Parable" here means the material exemplification of an obscure conceptual meaning. We do not know what possessed Hooper to put on the veil. It is not even certain that he knows himself. The origin of his act is absent, unattainable, just as our own conception, birth, or where we were before conception is unavailable to us. If what Hooper does comes without preparation or ascertainable cause into Milford, what happens thereafter is the prolonged repetition of the initial instant in which nothing happens except the proffering of an enigmatic sign. Hooper appears wearing the veil. He goes on wearing the veil until death and beyond death. All that happens in the story is one unsuccessful attempt after another to interpret the veil. Just as no mortal can make death the object of present experience, so the unveiling that Hooper promises never occurs in this world. Hooper is buried a veiled corpse, and his face moulders to dust beneath the veil.

The heterogeneity of a historical happening, its differentiation within itself, its contamination by an other than itself that is not outside in opposition to it but within, may be discerned both "horizontally" and "vertically". On the one hand, this heterogeneity is present in the "vertical" discrepancy between the posited material base, in this case the piece of folded black crape of which the veil is made, and the parabolic meaning revealed and at the same time veiled by the material sign. On the other hand, the heterogeneity is present in the demonstration that human life is both finite and unbounded. To be human is to be destined to die, to be inhabited by a mortality we can neither possess nor know, since it lies outside the borders of birth and death. These two forms of self-division are versions of one another, since what the veil expresses parabolically is just that forever unattainable blankness before birth and beyond the tomb—an unnamable "it".

The performative effect *of* the story, and of its parabolic expression, what happens *in* the story, can be even more exactly defined. My entitling sequence goes from theory to example to reading of that example to history, now defined as the unpredictable performative effect of signs when they are read. The theory in this case is the formulation by Hawthorne himself and by James after him of an unfortunate discrepancy in Hawthorne's tales. There is an apparently remediable division between material base, that is, realistic story, and ideological superstructure, that is, allegorical meaning. The reading of the story has shown that this disjunction between meaning and carrier of meaning may be not a remediable discrepancy but an ineluctable necessity. Moreover, the story redefines the disjunction in a way that displaces it, reworks it. The first disjunction disappears within an even more radical separation, that between any sign whatsoever and a meaning that is not momentarily absent, but wholly unreachable. Such a meaning is the radical other of a sign that appears to gesture toward it and at the same time permanently veils it.

Hawthorne's story operates as a powerful critique of the assumption that the cleft between realism and allegory is contingent. The story shows that this disjunction is not accidental (product of Hawthorne's deficiencies as a writer, or of his psychological peculiarities, or of his life experience, or of the thinness and blankness of American culture), but necessary and universal. It is an essential feature of any historical happening anywhere, even in England, for example, with all its thickness of historical and social complexity. The theoretical distinction between allegory and realism with which I began has been dissolved by the reading of the story. In this case too it must be said that reading is the displacement of theoretical hypotheses rather than their confirmation.

In place of the theoretical hypothesis with which I began is put a new theoretical proposition that may be expressed in either of two ways. The real material sign, the piece of black crape, is so empty of ascertainable meaning or so distant from the meaning for which it stands that it is rather a catachrestic expression of the unattainability of allegorical meaning than the sign for a meaning with which it is incommensurate. The most successful allegorical signs are those, like the black veil, that resist successfully any conceptual formulation of their meaning. This is so even though they appear to demand such an interpretation, and even though we make the most strenuous efforts to lift the veil. The black veil is a black veil, a piece of black crape. "The Minister's Black Veil" means what it says, no more, no less. It does not respond to any of our attempts to read it. Those flat historical notations in Hawthorne's notebooks, about which Henry James complained, are, one might argue, the most successfully allegorical words he ever wrote. Hawthorne's failure to express allegorical meanings in his novels and tales, their tendency to fade to blank pages in the sunlight, is their triumph. The distinction between realistic and allegorical narratives disappears in a sign that is at once blankly realistic and at the same time absolutely allegorical, that is, a sign for the failure of allegory.

But there is even more to say of the way the reading of "The Minister's Black Veil", like its writing, printing, and publishing, are paradigmatic historical events. The reading of the story, both as the mere passing of the words through the mind of the reader and as strenuous critical reflection on those words, is a historical event, wherever and whenever it occurs, for example for you and me now. This happening has a double definition. On the one hand reading, for example the reading of "The Minister's Black Veil", is a powerful instrument for the dismantling of ideological mystifications. In this case the mystifications are the assumed opposition between realism and allegory and the

Puritan ideology of apocalypse associated with the figure of the veil.

The most elegant and succinct formulation of this indispensable function of theoretical reading is proposed by Paul de Man in a well-known passage in "The Resistance to Theory". "What we call ideology", says de Man, "is precisely the confusion of linguistic with natural reality, of reference with phenomenalism. It follows that, more than any other mode of inquiry, including economics, the linguistics of literariness is a powerful and indispensable tool in the unmasking of ideological aberrations, as well as a determining factor in accounting for their occurrence. Those who reproach literary theory for being oblivious to social and historical (that is to say ideological) reality are merely stating their fear at having their own ideological mystifications exposed by the tool they are trying to discredit. They are, in short, very poor readers of Marx's *German Ideology*."[20] Certainly my reading of "The Minister's Black Veil" would exemplify this claim for an indispensable social function of "rhetorical reading". I have shown that Hawthorne's story does not merely reaffirm the Puritan version of the traditional language of parable and apocalypse, that is, the notion that here below, in this mortal life, each of us veils a secret sin that will be unveiled at the general resurrection. At the same time, such a reading shows, the story puts that ideology in question. In doing that, the story functions as a powerful uprooting of the ideology of an opposition between realism and allegory on which Hawthorne's self-analysis and deliberate procedures as a writer depend.

But the reader should always be wary when such a claim of mastery through a happy marriage of theory and reading is made. In the context of my own reading here, there is something a little too reassuring about calling rhetorical reading a "tool". That sounds as though it were something, a technique or a procedure, a reader could control and freely manipulate. In the light of this essay, the latent or effaced prosopopoeia in the word "unmasking" is also a little unsettling. Rhetorical reading is a "tool" for "unmasking"! That seems to contradict what I have, with the help of Hawthorne, said about the possibility of the impossibility of unmasking.

The reader might be alerted by a certain slippage in the sentences I have quoted from de Man. He begins by praising rhetorical reading, calling it a "mode of inquiry" into "the linguistics of literariness", elsewhere in the essay defined as "the rhetorical or tropological dimension of language" (RT, 17). This then slides into a defense not of reading but of theory as such. The whole point of de Man's intricate argument, however, is to move through the assertion that "the resistance to theory is in fact a resistance to reading" (15) to a final much more radical assertion that rhetorical reading and literary theory, far from being in happy harmony, are in irreconcilable opposition. Rather than facilitating reading, theory, even the theory of rhetorical reading, contaminates, inhibits, and ultimately disables rhetorical reading. "Technically correct rhetorical readings", says de Man at the very end of his essay, "may be boring, monotonous, predictable and unpleasant, but they are irrefutable . . . They are, always in theory, the most elastic theoretical and dialectical model to end all models and they can rightly claim to contain within their own defective selves all the other defective models of reading-avoidance, referential, semiological, grammatical, performative, logical, or whatever. They are theory and not theory at the same time, the universal theory of the impossibility of theory. To the extent however that they are theory, that is to say teachable, generalizable and highly responsive to systematization, rhetorical readings, like the other kinds, still avoid and resist the reading they advocate. Nothing can overcome the resistance to theory since theory *is* itself this resistance" (*RT*, 19).

Surely, in spite of de Man's warning that the resistance to reading cannot be resisted, I can avoid this danger, now that I know all about it, with the help of Hawthorne, James, and de Man. In this case too lucid knowledge of the truth should set me free. But can we not see, in retrospect, an example of a distressing asymmetry between theory and reading in the reading I have proposed here of "The Minister's Black Veil"? Have I not, not through some remediable inadvertence or forgetting, but through an ineluctable compulsion, unavoidably used as the "tool" of reading the very thing I have most wanted to put in question, just that ideology of apocalypse with its associated figures of the veil and of prosopopoeia? Have I not all along projected a human face, a personality and a voice into those little black marks on the page, marks as dead as any corpse or stone? Just as surely as the citizens of Milford projected a face behind the black veil of the Reverend Hooper and assumed that the missing face was an index of a personality behind the veiling mask of the face, so have I projected faces, selves, and voices on the white pages, filigreed in black. I have thought of the "Hawthorne" or of "James" I reach through the printed page as real people. I have personified a whole epoch in the name of Benjamin Franklin. Most of all, I have written of Hooper and of his fellow parishioners as if they too were real people, though they have no existence beyond the marks on the page.

I cannot read the story without doing this, even though the point of the story is to put in question the activity of prosopopoeia on which its functioning as a narrative depends. By the time I have, with the help of the story, come to doubt the validity of such personifying projections, it is too late to go back. I have already committed the crime I am led by the story to condemn. I have been made the mystified victim, once more, of the piece of ideology I would "unmask". I have done this as surely now, through the act of reading "The Minister's Black Veil", as when I was a child I used to think of the characters in the children's books I read, *Alice in Wonderland* or *Swiss Family Robinson*, as having somewhere a real and perpetually continuing existence. The reading of the books gave me momentary access to those secret worlds, like going through a window or passing through a mirror into another land.

Even the most sophisticated reading of "The Minister's Black Veil" is a permutation of this primitive and infantile infatuation. In order to demystify, "unmask", I must forget that I am using as the "tool" of unmasking the thing I am unmasking, the trope of personification. In order to read the story as a critique of the ideology opposing realism to allegory, and of the ideology of apocalyptic unveiling, I must reaffirm the ideology from which I want to free myself and my readers. This is the stubborn presupposition that behind every mask there is a face, and behind every face, as behind every sign or configuration of signs, there is somewhere a personality, a self, a subject, a transcendental ego. Belief in the truth value of the figure of prosopopoeia is an ideological construct so basic that it is hard to imagine a workable human society without it.

The violence of my reading as a historical event has depended on prosopopoeia in another, more hidden, more radical, more rooted, way. Have I not written of the patient text, enduring and silent, like Melville's Bartleby, or, like Bartleby, speaking in a way that puts a stop to all verifiable hermeneutical affirmation? The text too, I have argued, answers "I should prefer not to", to all the interpretative hypotheses we propose to it. To speak in this way personifies not Hooper or Hawthorne, but the text itself, just as de Man personifies ideology as something present in texts that rhetorical reading can "unmask". Such prosopopoeias are so natural, so surreptitious, so much a part of ordinary language, as to go without saying. They pass almost unnoticed. This instinctive personifying of texts, even more than thinking of characters in stories as real persons, justifies saying that prosopopoeia is a fundamental feature of historical events as happenings.

History, I now conclude, is an endless series of disruptive happenings. Each repeats, in one way or another, the linguistic error of personifying the absent, the inanimate, or the dead. Each imposes or projects a face on the veil, or creates a face that acts as a veil. In such projections we repeat the discrepancy between ideology and the material base even in the act of "unmasking" it. To put this another way, the working of my reading, like the working of Hawthorne's parable, is a speech act. Like all speech acts, my reading is a historical happening. Just as a parable is not a description but an act of language that works to divide the sheep from the goats, those who have eyes and see from those who do not, though there is no certain way to decide which of those groups you are in, so my reading will work to make something happen in those who read or hear it, but that effect will be unpredictable. This means that I have provided yet another example of theory as the resistance to reading, since my reading depends on using the piece of mystification I want "theoretically" to "unmask".

I ask, finally, who is this "I" who speaks or writes here? Who is this "we" in whose name I have frequently spoken? Who speaks, reads, or writes in this case, who "performs" into existence the historical events I have been discussing? By what authority, in whose name, are all these signs proffered? The question can be asked of Hawthorne as the author of the tale, of Hooper as the one who puts forth the sign of the black veil, and of "me" as the author of this essay. By what authority, in whose name, did Hawthorne rework with such interpretative violence the materials of New England history? By what authority, in whose name, did Hooper decide one day to begin wearing his black veil? By what authority, in whose name, did I decide to write an essay on Hawthorne's "The Minister's Black Veil" and then follow the trajectory to which that decision led me?

These questions may be clarified by an analogy to what St Paul says about speaking in tongues. "If any man speak in an unknown tongue", says Paul, "let it be by two, or at the most by three, and that by course [that is, one person at a time]; and let one interpret" (1 Corinthians 14:27). Any literary text is something like a speaking in tongues in the sense that it is always to some degree enigmatic, puzzling. There needs to be one to interpret – a reader, teacher, or critic who can say with authority what the speaking in tongues means. But the authorizing source of any glossolalia is always in doubt. Is it from God or is it from the devil? In a similar way, the authenticity of any literary text remains in doubt until some authoritative reader or critic has interpreted it and testified to its provenance and authenticity, given it the stamp of approval, so to speak. But the question of authority then displaces itself. How are we to be sure that the "one who interprets" knows what he is talking about and translates accurately the speaking in tongues so all who listen may know?

The answers to my questions about "The Minister's Black Veil" are easy to give. The putting in question, suspension, or "deconstruction" of the truth value of prosopopoeia performed by the story and repeated in one way or another in any reading of it, while at the same time the prosopopoeia is in one way or another necessarily reaffirmed, must occur for Hawthorne, for Hooper, and for any reader, including "me". In the reading act the "I" that seems to use "theory" as an indispensable tool to unmask ideology is dispossessed. It is deprived of its authority as a pre-existing origin. The "I" becomes a linguistic function in a process that occurs of its own accord and is authorized by no independent witnessing "I". It is not an "I" who speaks or writes, in any of these effectively working historical actions. It is an impersonal possibility of thinking, speaking, and writing, there already within language, that takes possession of the "I" to think itself, speak itself, or write itself and thereby enters into history. When it enters history it makes things happen there as they happen. The ethics of reading, "I" have once more discovered, is this impersonal response to an implacable and impersonal demand, not the response of a freely willing and choosing I to alternative possibilities in the light of some ethical norm or scale of values. At the same time, however, by an equally inescapable necessity, in any of these reading or writing acts unmasking prosopopoeia the illusory sovereign "I" is in one way or another at the same time reposited, and that "I" must in its own proper name take responsibility for the results of its acts of reading, writing, or speaking. "I" did it, and I must take the consequences.

"I" draw the following conclusions from what I have said. As long as the relation between text and context, literature and history, is defined in one way or another in grammatical or logical terms, that is, as the control of one linguistic code over another set of signs, the traditional assumption that history causes literature or that literature merely reflects history will have reasserted itself in another guise. This will happen in spite of claims by the interpreter that he or she has made the "linguistic turn". Only a rhetorical analysis of the relation between literature and history, an analysis recognizing the relation to be tropological, not merely conventional, grammatical, or logical, will escape some more or less subtle reaffirmation of historical determinism.

Moreover, only the recognition that a work of literature, in its production and in its reading, is a speech act, performative as well as constative, will escape from the reassertion in one way or another of the priority of history over literature. This means that a scrupulous analysis of the way speech acts work is a fundamental part of literary study today.

Discussions of theory, finally, should center not on the conceptual validity of this or that theory as such, but on the ways a given theory facilitates reading. Reading here is meant in an extended sense. It means not just reading literary works, but reading historical documents, works of art, material artifacts, cultural signs of all sorts. Such signs are transmitted from the past and permeate our lives today in ever-renewed memorial acts of reading that make history.

NOTES

1 *L'écriture du désastre* (Paris: Gallimard, 1980) pp. 102–3.
2 See Jane Tompkins, "Masterpiece Theater: The Politics of Hawthorne's Literary Reputation", *Sensational Designs: The Cultural Work of American Fiction: 1790–1860* (Oxford: Oxford University Press, 1985) pp. 3–39 for an admirable account of the process whereby Hawthorne's work became canonized. Tompkins includes "The Minister's Black Veil" among the works now considered to be one of "his great short stories" (p. 10), but she observes that in Hawthorne's own day sketches like "Little Annie's Rambles" and "A Rill from the Town Pump" were more highly valued. Tompkins's chapter is a test case for arguing that "changing definitions of literary value, institutionally and socially produced, continually refashion the literary canon to suit the culture's needs" (p. 34). I ask rather whether it is possible that the act of reading might escape from the "interpretive frame" enclosing the reader when he or she opens the book. My recent work argues through a series of examples that reading, when it occurs, which is not all that often, does go against the grain of theoretical assumptions or presupposed "interpretive frames". Reading and theory are asymmetrical. Reading may be radically inaugural and therefore politically and ethically initiatory. Much hangs on a decision between these two views of the social function of literature.
3 Henry James, *Hawthorne*, in Leon Edel and Mark Wilson (ed.), *Literary Criticism: Essays on Literature: American Writers; English Writers* (New York: The Library of America, 1984) pp. 351–2, henceforth "J", followed by the page number.
4 Readers of "Ethan Brand" will know that the image of the dog chasing its tail, far from being meaningless, becomes in that story a figure for that inturning of consciousness on itself that constitutes the "unpardonable sin" in Brand.

5   James's distaste for Hawthorne's "allegory" remains a com-
monplace of twentieth-century criticism of Hawthorne. See,
for example, R. P. Blackmur's Afterword to *"The Celestial
Railroad" and Other Stories* in James T. Jones (ed.), *Outsider
at the Heart of Things: Essays by R. P. Blackmur* (Urbana:
University of Illinois Press, 1989) pp. 266–73. "I find", says
Blackmur, "that in these remarks I have repeated a good
many times different versions of the judgment of Hawthorne
which I now bring to a head when I say that his allegory is
reductive, as if allegory could go backward, and is even
more likely to do so in him than to go forward" (p. 273).
Blackmur's essay was first published in 1963.

6   Roy Harvey Pearce (ed.), *Tales and Sketches* by Nathaniel
Hawthorne (New York: The Library of America, 1982)
p. 975. Henceforth, citations from this volume will be indicated by page numbers alone.

7   R. P. Blackmur, Afterword to *"The Celestial Railroad" and
Other Stories* ed. cit., pp. 266–73.

8   See Michael J. Colacurcio, "The True Sight of Sin: Parson
Hooper and the Power of Blackness", *The Province of Piety:
Moral History in Hawthorne's Early Tales* (Cambridge: Har-
vard University Press, 1984) pp. 314–85, for the fullest
commentary on this story in its historical context. Other
discussions of "The Minister's Black Veil" include: Richard
H. Fogle," 'An Ambiguity of Sin and Sorrow' ", *The New
England Quarterly* 21, no. 3 (September, 1948) pp. 342–9;
Gilbert P. Voigt, "The Meaning of 'The Minister's Black
Veil' ", *College English* 13, no. 6 (March, 1952) pp. 337–8;
William Bysshe Stein, "The Parable of the AntiChrist in
'The Minister's Black Veil' ", *American Literature* 27, no. 3
(November 1955) pp. 386–92; Robert W. Cochran, "Haw-
thorne's Choice: The Veil or the Jaundiced Eye", *College
English* 23, no. 5 (February 1962) pp. 342–6; George Mon-
teiro, "Hawthorne's 'The Minister's Black Veil' ", *The Expli-
cator* 22, no. 2 (October, 1963) item 9; Nicholas Canaday,
Jr., "Hawthorne's Minister and the Veiling Deceptions of
Self", *Studies in Short Fiction* 4, no. 2 (Winter, 1967)
pp. 135–42; Frederick W. Turner, III, "Hawthorne's Black
Veil", *Studies in Short Fiction* 5, no. 2 (Winter, 1968)
pp. 186–7; Raymond Benoit, "Hawthorne's Psychology of

Death: 'The Minister's Black Veil'", *Studies in Short Fiction* 8, no. 4 (Fall, 1971) pp. 553–60; Robert E. Morsberger, "'The Minister's Black Veil': Shrouded in a Blackness, Ten Times Black", *The New England Quarterly* 46, no. 3 (September, 1973) pp. 454–63; Glenn C. Altschuler, "The Puritan Dilemma in 'The Minister's Black Veil'", *American Transcendental Quarterly*, 24, suppl. 1 (1974) pp. 25–7; James B. Reece, "Mr Hooper's Vow", *ESQ* 21 (1975) pp. 93–102; Lawrence I. Berkove, "'The Minister's Black Veil': The Gloomy Moses of Milford", in C. E. Frazer Clark, Jr. (ed.), *The Nathaniel Hawthorne Journal, 1978* (Detroit: Gale Research Company, 1984) pp. 147–57; Rosemary F. Franklin, "'The Minister's Black Veil': A Parable", *American Transcendental Quarterly* 56 (1985) pp. 55–63.

9 Though the modern reader has no way to know this from the story itself, the Reverend Moody of York, Maine, was a real person. Bliss Carnochan of Stanford University first gave me leads to follow on this. Carnochan has provided me with xeroxes from a family diary referring to a several-times-great-grandfather of his, William Farnham (b. 1766?), whose father was "prepared for college" by the Reverend Moody, known as "Handkerchief Moody", and who as a child once peeped under Moody's handkerchief. This occurred when Moody was a visitor in Farnham's parents' household and was leading family prayers: "he [William Farnham] seized the opportunity, when the good man was fervently engaged in his petitions, to creep slowly, and cautiously along, and peep under the mysterious handkerchief". The diary confirms that Moody had indeed shot by accident "a lad of his acquaintance". He was known as "Handkerchief Moody" because he "never appear[ed] in the last years of his life without his face being covered by a handkerchief." Moody himself kept in his earlier years (1720–1724) a diary, written in Latin and set down in a substitution cipher. Virginia S. Woodwell, of York, Maine, has been kind enough to provide me with a copy of *Handkerchief Moody: The Diary & the Man*, decoded, translated, and interpreted by Philip McIntire Woodwell (Portland: Colonial Offset Printing Co., 1981). This contains much valuable information. Carnochan has published an excellent essay on

Hawthorne's story: "'The Minister's Black Veil': Symbol, Meaning, and the Context of Hawthorne's Art", *Nineteenth-Century Fiction*, 24, no. 2 (September, 1969) pp. 182–92. Carnochan's essay, however, though it mentions the Reverend Moody, does not discuss the family diary, since he did not yet know about it when he wrote his essay. I am grateful to Professor Carnochan for permission to refer to this material.

10   See Franz Kafka, *Parables and Paradoxes*, in German and English (New York: Schocken Books, 1971) pp. 10–11. For a discussion of Kafka's little text and of the differences between sacred and secular parable see my "Parable and Performative in the Gospels and in Modern Literature", in Gene M. Tucker and Douglas Knight (eds.), *Humanizing America's Iconic Book* (Chico, California: Scholar's Press, 1982), pp. 57–71.

11   Edgar Allan Poe, "*Twice-Told Tales* by Nathaniel Hawthorne", *Essays and Reviews* (New York: The Library of America, 1984) pp. 574–5.

12   D. A. Miller, "The Administrator's Black Veil: A Response to J. Hillis Miller", *ADE Bulletin*, no. 88 (Winter, 1987) p. 50.

13   Gerard Manley Hopkins, in Claude Colleer Abbott (ed.), *The Letters . . . to Robert Bridges* (London: Oxford University Press, 1955) p. 270.

14   See Jacques Derrida, *D'un ton apocalyptique adopté naguère en philosophie* (Paris: Galilee, 1983) pp. 11–16.

15   Paul de Man, "Autobiography as De-Facement", *The Rhetoric of Romanticism* (New York: Columbia University Press, 1984) p. 81.

16   I have discussed Melville's story in *Versions of Pygmalion* (Cambridge: Harvard University Press, 1990) pp. 141–78.

17   I have discussed this issue, apropos of Kleist's "Über die allmähliche Verfertigung der Gedanken beim Reden", in *Versions of Pygmalion*.

18   John E. Toews, "Intellectual History after the Linguistic Turn: The Autonomy of Meaning and the Irreducibility of Experience", *The American Historical Review* 92, no. 4 (October, 1987) pp. 879, 881–2, 885, 886.

19   Herman Melville, "Hawthorne and His Mosses", in Harri-

son Hayford (ed.), *Pierre: Israel Potter: The Piazza Tales: The Confidence Man: Uncollected Prose: Billy Budd, Sailor* (New York: The Library of America, 1984) p. 1165.

20 Paul de Man, "The Resistance to Theory", *The Resistance to Theory* (Minneapolis: University of Minnesota Press, 1986) p. 11. Further references to this volume will be identified as "RT", followed by the page number.

The Authority of Reading:
An Interview with J. Hillis Miller

conducted by Martin Heusser and Harold Schweizer

HEUSSER We'll start with the end first. Beginning with the beginning might be an illusion, and therefore the first question is the following: Finally, should we not admit that in the absence of metaphysical certitudes, we must ethically commit ourselves to those certainties which for the moment, at the least, are functional, utilitarian, or even humanitarian. In order to act, as Nietzsche's Hamlet doctrine puts it, we must have illusions, but why shouldn't we?

MILLER If you act on the basis of illusions, the results are not certain to be disastrous, but they probably have a greater chance of being disastrous than if they are on the basis of the truth. That would be my answer to that. I would be happier if those humanitarian principles were ones we could be certain about, for example the sanctity of life, something that you might defend because it has some kind of truth. The problem with saying, "I know all these values are illusions, nevertheless you have to act according to some kind of consensus about goods in the given society", is that it's a very risky thing to do. Riskier than to act in terms of the best view you can get of the truth. You might argue, for example, that we really know the CO_2 is going to raise the temperature of the planet, but the social chaos that would result from accepting this truth would be so great that it's really better to go on acting and planning, making political and ethical decisions, as though the Antarctic ice cap were not going to melt. I think that would be a mistake, and I take that as an emblematic example of my answer to the question.

HEUSSER   So, you would not subscribe to the idea entertained by the deconstructionist of a beginning or starting point as illusion?

MILLER   No. I don't think that's what "deconstructionists" say. Let's step back a moment and see if we can agree to talk about not just any ethical situation, decision, or action, but a particular one, namely one involving reading. You can generalize on that and say all ethical acts and decisions, or all political acts and decisions, take place in situations of reading, but you have to take reading metaphorically in order to say that. So let's say, when we're talking about deconstruction, whatever that is – I would prefer to say "deconstructionisms" – we're talking about a reading situation. The reader has not an illusory but specific and concrete starting point, namely the text. Nothing could be more real than that. It's so many sheets of paper with black marks on them, though such material objects may generate many illusions and many truths too. It's not a matter of a perspective that you arbitrarily take. You start with the event of reading, which is neither illusory nor arbitrary, but is something that occurs when you read, and you go on from there. The notion that the starting point is arbitrary or illusory or merely perspectival is not, in my view, correct. That would be my answer.

I understand the point of the question you're asking and what it has to do with the first question you asked. The ethical, political, and historical implications of the act of reading are disquieting. Reading is somehow freed from those community values that you were talking about at the beginning. It suspends them or may be outside them. At the same time the event of reading is itself a grounding. What happens when you read happens, and one has to go on from there. That's what I mean by saying it's an event, to some degree a disruptive event. I don't think anything is gained by pretending otherwise, by claiming that reading simply reinforces values or judgements the reader already has.

SCHWEIZER   But doesn't deconstruction tell us that our actions have no higher authority or cannot be authorized in any other than in a particular historical or contextual way? In other words, don't we have to understand our ethics as an ethics of the moment? Don't we act without any other authority than the kind of authority we derive from a particular reading event, that is, from the particular interpretation of any particular situation?

MILLER   I have three things to say about that. First, I would more or less accept what you've said, that is, I"d stress the specificity, uniqueness, nonrepeatability of the reading event. I would agree with you that the authority of reading comes only from that. That's one of the things I mean by saying that the authority of reading is a disruptive authority. It's not controllable by the various forms of prediction or containment that one might wish to use. That's my quarrel with reader-response criticism. It says reading is controlled by some community of readers. That would allow you to predict that such and such a reader within a certain historical community and institutional context would read *Paradise Lost* in a certain way. My claim is that that's not the case with real reading. Each act of reading is unique. It makes a unique call or demand on the reader. That call I must answer, even if it is only to say no, to refuse it, as with a collect long-distance telephone call. "Do you accept the charges?" "No. I refuse."

My second response to your question is to say that I disagree with Nietzsche. Nietzsche says there are certain truths mankind cannot stand. They are true, but they're incompatible with going on. I understand the force of that. It's a radical claim that arouses my instinctive sympathy. What follows from this, however, is that we should therefore allow, coach, institutionalize in the community certain nontruths. But the losses involved in doing that are so great that I would find myself saying, "No, humankind is strong enough to live with whatever is the truth, or they had better be." So I disagree with Nietzsche on that point, though I understand the force of it.

The third point is a little more difficult to make. Your question suggests that the authority of that moment is entirely *sui generis*, and, in that sense, something that you can't really do anything with. It seems to be an authority without authority, as Blanchot might say. Let me try to explain what I mean by the authority of that moment when I read *What Maisie Knew, Middlemarch*, or some other work of literature. I speak for the moment of acts of reading literary works rather than of other analogous acts of reading, like reading historical texts, or reading other people, or reading political situations. The authority that comes to me, that is, the obligation that I incur through the reading event, is not simply the authority of the text as a collection of words on the page and the meaning that they have for me when I read. What calls to me, makes demands on me, is something else, something that I would call "other", something that this particular text gives me access to. That "other" is the real source of authority that allows me then to say, or obligates me to say, "I must do so and so". The preface to *The Golden Bowl* by James is important for me because it allowed me to understand that. There are other places to understand it, or where I think I have understood it, for example Kafka's parable, "Before the Law". If I understand James, he's saying that when he reread *The Golden Bowl*, what had authority over him in revising it was not some arbitrary decision on his part to alter the text for the purpose of clarity or because he would write it differently now. That is to say, James's reading was not a matter of "reader-response". Reading *The Golden Bowl* gave James access again to that which the text was authorized by. His figure for that is a great expanse of untrodden snow. His reconfrontation of that had authority over him to make revisions.

Something similar is a theme in Derrida that is not often talked about. It's almost impossible to talk about without sounding mystical, misty, vague, or metaphysical. Another place where I've encountered something similar is Benjamin's essay on translation. Benjamin speaks of the test and the translation as being equally distant from another text which can never be given. He calls it the pure speech, "die reine Sprache", of which the original text is already a translation. This pure speech is "other" in relationship to any version of it. That corresponds to what happens when I respond to the reading of a particular work of literature with the sense that there's something that I'm authorized to do, something that I must do in my own life, that I've learned to do by that work. Now, the actual implementation of that decision, politically, institutionally, ethically, may not turn out to have the effects that I would wish it to have. But this is another matter, another dimension. Perhaps other questions you'll ask will bear on that question.

Kleist in "On the Gradual Fabrication of Thoughts while Speaking" proposes the figure of "the workshop of the imagination", a weaving image. While you're talking some other part of you is thinking for you, weaving thoughts. Kleist's essay has to do not so much with the authority given to me by the act of reading as with the question of what happens then in the real world when the result of my reading enters the world of history, other people, and so on. That is by no means a straight line. You cannot say, for example, that you learn from James's *What Maisie Knew*, or from James generally, that renunciation is the highest virtue, and that you can therefore be sure that you or I in our own real lives would produce peace and happiness all around us by renouncing. You learn from James that renunciation is the highest virtue, all right. We should all be like Maisie or like Milly Theale or like Strether and renounce. But what the novels show and what I think real life shows is the following: these people in James's novels act correctly. They do the right thing, ethically the correct thing. In that sense they are models to be followed. But the novels do not tell the reader exactly what that would mean in a particular case that you or I might be in. That we must figure out for ourselves, as Maisie, Millie, and Strether did. James's novels also show that the effects of proper ethical action are by no means benign in the real world. The spectacular example is Maggie's condoning of the adultery of Charlotte and Maggie's husband in *The Golden Bowl*. Maggie refuses to acknowledge that she knows about her husband's infidelity. She renounces her privilege as an injured wife. That renunciation keeps her marriage and that of her father to Charlotte together. This seems to be good in every way, except that it has an absolutely devastating effect on the lives of both the Prince and Charlotte. It condemns the Prince to spend the rest of his life in American City, and it condemns the Prince and Charlotte to be separated forever. Maggie does the right thing, but its implementation in the real world by no means brings happiness.

I've just finished rereading James's *The Wings of the Dove*. I've spoken of Milly Theale, but the real person who renounces there is Densher. He gives up the money. Milly does make an act of sacrifice; she sacrifices her life and leaves all her money to Densher. The effect of that good, almost saintly, act – she turns her face to the wall and dies so that Densher can have the money and marry the woman he really loves – the effect of that is to separate them forever. The novel ends with Kate and Densher separated. But Densher also makes a renunciation, and the word "renunciation" is used for what he does. The name in that novel for that authorizing "other" is "death", the death of Milly. Kate quite correctly says "you're in love with her memory", that is, the memory of Milly. That is a very odd notion. How can you be in love not with a person but with the memory of that person after his or her death? The novel ends, you'll remember, when he says, "I will marry you in an hour", and she asks, "As we were?" that is, if we go back to where we were before Milly died and left you the money. He replies, "As we were", and she says, "We shall never again be as we were". An irrevocable difference has been made by Milly's death. That's as good a name as any for this "other" I'm talking about, something other than any explicit thematic meaning that literature gives you access to.

HEUSSER   How does that relate to the somewhat old-fashioned idea of the *au delà du tombeau*?

MILLER   My only way of understanding this is to read poems and novels that talk about it. The trouble with *au delà du tombeau* is that it suggests that death is somewhere beyond in some "over there", whereas the lesson that James's novel seems to give is that death is there all the time. It cannot be located either as an origin and a beginning, a darkness that precedes narrative, nor as something that is going to happen in the future, nor as a kind of punctuation that occurs somewhere in the middle. It's a pervasive constant presence that cannot be named except in some kind of catachresis. There's a marvellous moment in *The Wings of the Dove* which in a way expresses that. James, speaking for Densher, on pages 298–299 in the second volume of the New York edition, says, Densher saw that there was a conspiracy of silence around the fact that Milly was dying. Densher has a figure for this. He says, the "great smudge of mortality across the picture" – the general picture of her wonderful life – she has an enormous fortune; she can buy everything; she should be very happy, and she says she's happy – the smudge of mortality across that "received no reflection in spirit or in speech". Her mortality in no way was reflected in consciousness or in language. Then he says, "the mere aesthetic instinct of mankind –" he never finishes the phrase. The aesthetic, namely that which can be pictured, named, or experienced, what literature can be about, that is a "Schein" or appearance; the aesthetic in that sense, is the covering over of mortality, or the ignoring of it, or a conspiracy of silence about it. Mortality is one thing that cannot be spoken, that has no reflection in spirit or in speech. The aesthetic is here set against death. The mere aesthetic instinct is the instinct to reflect in no way or speak about the smudge of mortality, even though you could say that in James's novels the smudge of mortality is what the novels are all about. Or rather it might be better to say that, for James, there are three events that James doesn't register aesthetically, that is to say that are non-representable. All are versions of this "other" that I'm talking about that authorizes ethical actions while at the same time not in any straightforward way determining or defining them. One of the three is the moment of death. Milly's death is not described. It occurs offstage. We learn nothing definite about it. In fact we learn nothing directly about Densher's last interview with Milly, when he sees her once more in Venice after she's turned her face to the wall and is on her deathbed. That's not reported directly at all. The second thing for James that is not representable is sex. You could say that's a convention of the time, but I think it's more than that for James. Every reader of James's novels knows what happens; it's not a big secret. Almost all of them turn on some act of adultery or fornication. It's James's big subject. But it's something that cannot be directly named.

He's very explicit in *The Wings of the Dove* about the moment that Kate comes to Densher's rooms and sleeps with him. He says, "I've given you all sorts of things on my side, but you've given me nothing. I need some testimony to your fidelity." And she comes. She comes to his room, and we know what happens there. But it's not described; it's a blank place in the novel. The same thing can be said of the Prince's renewed adultery with Charlotte in *The Golden Bowl*. The third moment, the oddest one, is the moment of ethical decision, the moment of the actual ethical act or promise. A good example of the absence of that, because it's a very specific one, occurs in *The Princess Casamassima*. The three things that are not told in that novel are the three things that matter, that are the turning points of the novel. One of them is the weekend that Hyacinth spends with the Princess on her estate. This is duplicated by the same event with his best friend, who also apparently sleeps with the Princess. Hyacinth comes back transformed by this weekend, but it is a blank place in the narration. The second thing that's not described is Hyacinth's suicide. It's the culmination of the novel, but it's in no way described. You see it after the fact and before. The third thing that's not directly represented is the moment when Hyacinth makes the promise to the revolutionaries that he will do what they want him to do. That's the crucial moment of ethical commitment in the novel, and it's not represented. This is the most puzzling, because you say, why not? It seems like something you could talk about and that the narrator should narrate. One understands why the other two are omitted; why omit that moment of commitment? The implied reason is that the moment of ethical commitment is also somehow outside the aesthetic, outside the representable; it's like that great smudge of mortality or like sexual experience. Hyacinth's choice has political effects later on, when it's brought back into the world of history, time, ethical action, and so on, but in itself it is suspended or abstracted from them, just as death and sex are.

HEUSSER   This is a most interesting observation in view of the rhetoric of the obscene. As you know, the obscene, in Greek theatre, was not supposed to be shown onstage, and of course two out of these three . . .

MILLER   . . . sex and death . . .

HEUSSER   . . . were never shown. Now, what about the third, and what about the relation between, let's say James and the rhetoric of the obscene?

MILLER   Aristotle says the murder of Laius in *Oedipus the King* cannot be represented onstage. It has to take place offstage, as does the self-blinding of Oedipus at the end. These are examples he gives of things that should not be shown on the stage. And you might say that the second one is the moment of justice or ethical choice or decision. The other thing, of course, that is not shown is the bedding of Oedipus and Jocasta. That's the obscene which is absent. You wouldn't have expected that to be on the stage, although in Aristophanes there is plenty of obscenity on the stage, and of course *Oedipus the King* is obsessed throughout as much by incest as by parricide.

HEUSSER   But is there something that will make James and Aristotle declare these quantities as not-to-be-shown? I'm referring to something like the Law that you cannot show or the Ethics that you cannot represent.

MILLER   Yes, that is what the word "catachresis" I used earlier suggests. That they're not shown directly functions to indicate that they are not themselves. They stand for something else that is more fundamentally nonshowable, namely that otherness that gives the authority I was talking about. That would be the argument. Whether Aristotle meant that or not is hard to tell, but Aristotle was a very profound critic. At first you think what he means is, well, violence shouldn't be shown on the stage. But I think his prohibition indicates a deeper recognition of what actually is going on in that absence from the play. The question of whether the moment of ethical choice or decision can be shown seems to be answered in *Antigone*, where it *is* apparently shown. That's what the play is all about: Antigone deciding on the stage to go on not obeying Creon. But in fact her decision takes place before the play begins. It is the presupposition of Antigone's initial dialogue with her sister Ismene, that opens the play. So one would have to explore this a little further in Greek drama before generalizing about it. Kleist in his stories is willing to put on directly before you moments of extreme violence. In almost every story someone gets his brains dashed out, for example in "The Foundling", in *Michael Kohlhaas*, and in *The Earthquake in Chile*, the culmination of which is the dashing out of the brains of the baby, when it is thrown against the wall. It's a horrible scene. I think Kleist was quite deliberately defying Aristotle's prohibition. As with other aspects of Kleist, you could say he's got Aristotle in his mind. He's saying suppose we wrote something programmatically anti-Aristotelian?

HEUSSER That, by the way, is very ironic, because Piacchi in "The Foundling" is described to us as a man who can't father a child, and so Kleist is paying respect to that kind of taboo, whereas later on Piacchi is strong enough to dash out the brains of his adopted son.

MILLER Another one of the Aristotelian prohibitions that's defied is Aristotle's famous statement that literature ought to represent not just the possible but the probable, or likely. All of Kleist's stories tell of things that turn out to be circumstantially plausible but very improbable, horrible concatenations of unlikely circumstances, what he called "improbable veracities", "unwahrscheinliche

Wahrhaftigkeiten". Kleist is saying Aristotle was wrong; real life is in fact made up of improbabilities. If you want to be true to life, you have to show it is governed by things that are the most hideous and awful happenstances that don't appear to be things that our ordinary understanding of history or literature prepare us for. The distinction between literature and history, according to Aristotle, is that history is full of things that are improbable, that in fact really happened, whereas literature has got to show things that are likely and probable, because they're the general laws of the ways things happen. Kleist challenges that.

SCHWEIZER   Could we for a moment go back to *Antigone*? I just want to reconstruct my own understanding of what's been going on. In other words, if you're reading *Antigone* then, you would read at least parts of the plot as representing something unrepresentable. Do we really know what the play is all about? Why *does* Antigone decide not to obey Creon? Let us suppose Antigone's motives are suicidal, for reasons that she and we do not know. She acts under the illusion of fulfilling her familial and religious duties simply because these are comprehensible, traditional, classical, reasons for what she says and does. She fools everybody. She obeys only "the gods". But the gods are metaphors; they are the tropes of her own private and intimate reasons for doing what she would not do if she couldn't call her reasons "the gods".

MILLER   That's a very interesting reading of the play, and I wouldn't be able to add to it or put it in question, except to say it might be difficult to find textual evidence for your reading. But you should try to do so. I was thinking as you talked of the essays by Hölderlin on the Sophocles plays that he translated. I'm really changing the subject. Having said that I admire what you said, I'm talking about something slightly different to which your remarks led me. If you remember, Hölderlin says the *Antigone* and the *Oedipus* are held together by what he calls the "caesura", a suspension of the ongoing movement of the plot. He calls it an antirhythmic caesura, thinking of the plot as rhythmic in the Greek sense of *rhythmos*, as I understand it, meaning a kind of contour or shapeliness in time that makes a beginning, middle, and end. What Hölderlin says, in the "Remarks on *Oedipus*", is again a very anti-Aristotelian notion. He says that the beginning and end are kept apart by the caesura.[1] It's a weird notion. If it weren't for that caesura in the middle, the end and the beginning would come together like matter and anti-matter, and there would be no play. But that moment, a kind of suspension, is something that's against rhythm. It's a caesura in the technical prosodic sense of a break in the rhythm. It might also be thought of not as a moment that is not represented, but as a moment outside the rhythm and in that sense like those moments I was talking about that punctuate the James novels, moments that are not represented at all. In both *Oedipus* and *Antigone*, it's the speeches of the blind soothsayer, Teiresias, that Hölderlin describes as the moment of antirhythmic caesura in the plays. You could go on from what Hölderlin says to identify that moment as the instant of clairvoyance on the part of the blind soothsayer. Teiresias knows the beginning and the end, is both male and female, and so on. Oedipus's meeting with him is the moment in the play that gives him and the audience the nearest thing to direct access to that "otherness" that is motivating all the events and about which Oedipus has to be, until the very end, ignorant, in order for there to be a play. Something similar can be said for Creon's encounter with Teiresias in *Antigone*.

Hölderlin's radical interpretation of *Oedipus*, as you remember, proposes that Oedipus's error is an error of interpretation. It is the temerity of putting the facts together. On the basis of slender and not entirely conclusive evidence, he convicts himself of being the person who has killed Laius and slept with his mother Jocasta, and who therefore can be the person standing between man and the gods on whom the lightning of the gods can fall and so take away the curse on Thebes. His guilt, for Hölderlin, is not just the temerity of wishing to be the scapegoat, of saying I am the one, but also the temerity of interpretation. His fatal *hubris* is the desire to read the events and to make a story out of them. He wants to see clearly from beginning to end, which is just what Aristotle says a good story allows us to do. That's a stern warning for us readers. That's congruent with what I was saying earlier, that what happens when you read happens and you must take responsibility for it, even for its unforeseen political and ethical effects, for its effects in the real world.

SCHWEIZER When Oedipus stabs out his eyes, isn't that an appropriation of a responsibility that he wouldn't have to bear? Isn't that an act of hubris on his part, in the sense that he's saying: I want to understand this on my own terms, I want to understand this as my own doing, as it were, and not as a doing that, if I do not take responsibility for it, I will therefore not understand?

MILLER Putting out his eyes is a kind of symbolic castration, but he also destroys the power of seeing. He wants earlier to see, to see clearly how these events are held together, though others tell him, Teiresias especially, that it would be better not to know, and he violently rejects Teiresias's prophecy. I am attracted by those readings of the play, for example a splendid essay by Cynthia Chase, building on work by Sandor Gilman, that say the evidence is not absolutely conclusive. It requires putting together bits and pieces to make a not altogether justified whole. The text of the play as Sophocles wrote it has some ambiguity, particularly about the murder of Laius. There are two reports, one that says the murder was done by one person, the other by a band, and as Oedipus says, one person and a band just doesn't jibe. Oedipus chooses the one-person explanation because that's the one that convicts him. It's a classic detective story, but one in which the detective is the murderer. He's tracking down himself. It's the first and perhaps still the greatest of all detective stories. It has many images that are detective story clichés, in Conan Doyle for example, the image of tracing down the beast, and adding the footprints up to make a line. This is a figure for the narrative line that leads to the identification of the murderer.

HEUSSER You have repeatedly mentioned the religous dimension of writing. Would you enlarge on that point?

MILLER I'm anxious that what I have said not be taken in a straightforwardly religious sense. When I speak of the "other", this "otherness" should not be identified with god or some onto-theological "one". It would be wrong to say, "Ah, we know what he's talking about; he's talking about some transcendent otherness, and that's the religious side of Miller's thought". It's almost impossible to talk about "otherness" without being open to that kind of misunderstanding. I have no way of preventing that, except to say that I'm trying to talk about an experience of the "other" that remains within the entirely secular act of reading works of literature, works that are not sacred texts and that I would not wish to give the status of sacred texts.

There are certainly traces of my own Protestant heritage there in my insistence on the uniqueness, incommensurability, and privacy of the act of reading. But I think this is really only an analogy. Protestantism tends to emphasize, more than Catholicism is likely to do, the solitude and uniqueness of spiritual experience, the way it happens for me only. There are types of Catholicism that would have that. A Catholic might say, "You Protestants ought to come and join us, you would find that there's plenty of room for that." Nevertheless one knows that the idea that every man can be his own priest was fundamental to the Reformation at its inception. But I say that's only a kind of an analogy with what I've been saying about the encounter with the "other" in reading. A Protestant heritage might lead some-body who's interested in literature to be more inclined to think of the reading act as not amenable to being entirely policed by conventions of reading or the moment of history that I'm in.

So I'm interested in the moments when a novelty enters into the progression of history. I think it's good that so many people who are studying politics and literature now are especially interested in revolutionary moments, for example, the French Revolution. Revolution are moments when something happens that is not entirely predictable by what went before. The people who are the makers of a successful revolution are apparently always surprised when it works. That was true of the Russian Revolution. The people who made it were amazed when they found them-selves in power, so amazed that they remained confused for years. They just couldn't believe that this had happened. It took them quite a while to realize that they now had the responsibility of doing something.

My example of this from Kleist is the speech by Mira-beau in "The Gradual Fabrication of Thought while Speak-ing". He speaks in the parliament to the emissary from the king who has come to dismiss the parliament. At the beginning of his speech Mirabeau has no intention of caus-ing the French Revolution, but by the end of the speech he has caused it. The next thing he does is to change completely and now begin talking in a solemn, somber, businesslike way about what they have to do now. Those two moments in a revolution are really very different from one another. The first one happens to some degree fortuit-ously, at least if Kleist is right. The second one involves the taking of responsibility for what you've done but not done in the sense of having calculated it beforehand. The second does involve calculation.

If this paradigm is applied to reading literature, one might say that a real act of reading implicitly implies a rearrangement of the curriculum, the way English literature ought to be taught in my department, the humanities generally, and so on, however slight a rearrangement. The reading happens without thinking about that at all. Later on you say, "If I am right about this, then there ought to be the following changes", and you think about how you might go about making those. You take responsibility for what has happened. You say, "Well, we should hire another person in such and such a field, or we ought to have a seminar with the philosophy department on such and such", and so on. We can see this happening now at a moment which is relatively revolutionary, at least in this country, in the structure of humanities departments. For example, departments that some years ago would never have thought that they were going to need courses in theory at all, now decide that they have to have them. They plan how they can do it, get new appointments assigned, go out and hire people, run faculty seminars, get funding for that and so on. All of that, I'm saying, comes second. The really revolutionary moment had come earlier.

SCHWEIZER   Could I take this discussion in a somewhat different direction and ask you how compatible are historical methods of reading, such as a Marxist reading – how compatible would that be with the kind of reading you were advocating?

MILLER   I see this as a frontier of literary study now, to relate literature to history. The turn to history that is so evident everywhere is for the most part an admirable thing. It responds to a need to make the study of literature count in the real world. No reasonable person could deny that the study of the historical relations of literature is a good thing. One can measure in part the validity and the vitality of changes in literary study by the amount of intellectual energy that is liberated by them. Women's studies is remarkable for the amount of intellectual energy that has been freed to do good work by a new discipline. Earlier women were inhibited by a situation in which they were in a double-bind. If they played the game as it was set up by men, then they were simply reinforcing the male-dominated measure of things. If they didn't do that, they didn't have any role at all, because there was only that game to play. Now, with the possibility of studying women writers, rearranging the canon, doing all of the things that women's studies do, women have something that opens up a great avenue of intellectual action for them. I think the turn to history functions in somewhat the same way. A lot of people were prepared to do the difficult archival work that's required for serious study of the historical relations of literture. I applaud that. For example, the work that Greenblatt has done in Renaissance studies, or the substantial historical research that Catherine Gallagher has done in the field of the novel. In order to write the kind of books she wants to write, she has to go and learn a lot about Victorian history or seventeenth and eighteenth-century history and relate that to whoever she is writing about, Elizabeth Gaskell or Aphra Behn.

Having said that, I would say two further things: one, that this turn to history and the study of the historical context of literature in no way liberates anybody or releases any student of literature from the obligation to read the texts that are put back in the context, read in the serious sense of interpret, talk about in detail, etc. In fact it makes that operation all the more difficult, because you have to balance all you now know that earlier, other kinds of literary study indicated were not necessary to know. The implication in, say, F. R. Leavis's work is that you or I or anybody can read Dickens's *Hard Times* or other works in "the great tradition" without knowing much about the actual conditions of industrial life in Victorian England. We can evaluate Dickens's novel, read it and understand it. We don't have to know much history to do that. Or we can read D. H. Lawrence. Leavis was writing for an English public that more or less knew these facts. We have to recover them now, and the "new historicists" are calling that to our attention. Nevertheless, one of the reservations I have about their work is that they sometimes stop with the historical background. Some of the readings they give of the works are relatively unsatisfactory in the sense of being merely thematic. I'm not saying always. That's the first point.

The second point, equally important for me, is that the commitment to history in no way releases any scholar from the hard work of thinking out the theoretical questions involved. The first point had to do with reading. You've got to read Shakespeare. Having established this historical context, then you've got to say, what difference does this make for the way I read *King Lear*? And that means really reading *King Lear*, once again, doing it over again. The second question, however, is theoretical rather than a practical reading question. That is the question of how you formulate the relation between literature and history. Just saying, here is the context, there is the work: that's just the beginning of the question. That relationship is not a physical one, as might be suggested by the use of any kind of causal vocabulary. The relation is a text/text relation. The problematic of it has to do with language or other signs. I don't see why one should be afraid of that. I do know why. People say, "This is putting it all back into the realm of language; we're talking about real history." But the real history that we're dealing with here, however real it was, now has the form of pieces of language for us. It's not that the Battle of Waterloo didn't occur, but that anything we know about the Battle of Waterloo now is going to be historical traces that have the form of language or other signs. To relate *The Charterhouse of Parma* to the Battle of Waterloo is to relate it to those traces.

SCHWEIZER   But you seem to imply that there is something more real, or something prior to the text, when you compare literature to a historical background.

MILLER Words like "background" or "context" are not innocent. They beg all sorts of questions, though it's not that you could substitute more benign terms. There would be a long, long development necessary really to talk about this, but I have two simple things to say about it. One: the relationship between text and context is always figurative. Any conceivable vocabulary you have to talk about it is some figure of speech or other. Causality is a form of contiguity, post hoc propter hoc, and that's a mode of metonymy in one way or another. The notion that a literary work exemplifies history in the sense that it's like a lot of other things of the time is synecdoche, part for whole. The idea of representation, the figure of mirroring, is a powerful figure for the relation of literature to history. This notion that the work mirrors the context is metaphor. It says the work is like its surroundings. You have to choose among those various figures, whichever one you think is the appropriate one for a given case. That choice is not empirical. That's what I mean by saying it's not physical. It's a choice among rhetorical options for that relationship. That doesn't mean that it may not be true, but it has the kind of truth that a rhetorical or a textual statement can have, not the kind of truth that sentences like "The sun rose this morning", or "The temperature of the sun at the surface is so many degrees centigrade". It has a different kind of truth.

A final conviction, for me, is crucial here. Works of literature do not simply reflect or are not simply caused by their contexts. They have a productive effect in history. This can and should also be studied. To put this another way, the only thing that sometimes worries me about the turn to history now as an explanatory method is the implication that I can fully explain every text by its pre-existing historical context. But the publication of those works was itself a political or historical event that in some way or another changed history. I think that if you don't allow for that, then literature is not much worth bothering with. Why do I have to study *North and South* if all it does is to reflect the ideology, in however conflictual and complicated a way, that I could just as well learn by reading other historical documents? It must add something to them, to make the study of literature justified. It sometimes seems to me that some part of the motivation of the people who have made this turn to history and have invested so much energy in it is a desire to neutralize the historical power that literature has had, by explaining it away. If I can say, "What's *King Lear*? It's nothing more than a reflection of the ideology of Shakespeare's time", then in a sense I have neutralized *King Lear*. I have taken away from it any performative power that it might have had then, in a concrete way for the people who saw it then, or might have again now for you or me if we read it or see it on the stage. The distinction I'm making is between the constative or epistemological aspect of literature, that is, the way in which it provides knowledge in some way, and, on the other hand, the performative aspect. As long as you see literature as purely constative, as doing no more than making statements about the world, about the way things are, then it is capable of being reduced to reflection or representation. But as soon as you see in literature the performative aspect, the way the writing, publication, reading of a work of literature by anyone at any time makes something happen, in however small a way, then it has escaped from the control of its context. That goes back to what I've been saying about the *event* of reading and its uniqueness and the way it leads to inaugural change, however small.

SCHWEIZER   Is that why you attacked Marxist theorists in your MLA address?[2] Do they exert such a control through creating a historical context, when they fail (as you seemed to be saying) to acknowledge the rhetorical or figurative nature of their theoretical paradigms?

MILLER   I didn't intend to denigrate Marxist theory at all. That theory does seem to me, in many cases, to allow in one way or another for that performative dimension of literature. This is true in the work of both some older Marxists like Jameson and Eagleton, and also in the younger ones that I find very interesting, some of whom I cited in the MLA address. The latter are anxious in one way or another not to forget the rhetorical study of literature, let's say "deconstruction". They ask how you might do this study of the historical dimension of literature in light of that. I'm only now beginning to learn about Marxist criticism and have no quarrel with it. More generally I could say that such study has moved even since that MLA address quite a distance. The enterprise now called cultural criticism or cultural critique seems to me admirable and to be praised. It is conscious that the act of criticism, critique, or enlightenment, in which you identify something about a work of literature in the past, is at the same time a political action. Showing something as what it was has a political effect here and now. The self-conscious political motivation many cultural critics have is much more realistic than perhaps it used to be. Some critics make a kind of implausible jump. They say something like, "I'm a Marxist critic, therefore when I give a Marxist reading of *King Lear*, this is going to aid the dictatorship of the proletariat". The two activities seem so distant from one another that it is hard to see how you could get from one to the other. Much new work strikes me as much more politically sophisticated. It recognizes that literary study in a university, even in this country where it has relatively little effect, nevertheless does have political and social effects, but it makes more modest assumptions about those effects. The thinking about the institutionalizing of the study of literature that's going on now is often very good.

This would be a place to say that the constative and

performative dimensions of literature are asymmetrical, as de Man and Derrida have argued. In Foucault's later work, the relationship between knowledge and power, another way to talk about the constative/performative relation, is by no means straightforward and easy. Foucault's meditations about that relationship are subtle and persuasive. Insofar as the new historicists are good Foucauldians, which sometimes they may not be, they would find a basis in Foucault for recognizing what I am calling the performative power of literature. There is going to be a line from knowledge to the power-effect that that has, but it will not be direct. That's what Foucault is really saying, not that knowledge leads directly to power, or that knowledge is always an act of power, or that knowledge is empowering in some direct way.

I've been reading Adorno and Horkheimer's *Dialectic of Enlightenment* recently. That book is torn between two ways of thinking about this topic. One, that seems to me old-fashioned and wrong, sees knowledge leading directly to power, as Foucault is sometimes misread as saying. The other way of thinking, the real argument of that book, is more like the one that I'm making, namely that there is something in knowledge itself that leads to effects strangely askew when it's politically implemented. The essay on anti-semitism at the end of the book is one of the best essays, still, ever written on the question. It was written during the time that the Holocaust was going on, and written in California. I have some special interest in it since it's a California book. It was written in Los Angeles.

HEUSSER   You have always admitted to having changed your views on and approaches to literature.

MILLER   It would be boring, I think, if you didn't change. It's also compatible with my notion of the uniqueness of each act of reading, that is, what happens to me when I read. I've mentioned *What Maisie Knew*. Reading it was a good example of this for me. I wrote about fifty pages on *What Maisie Knew* three years ago. It was supposed to be a chapter for a new book, *Versions of Pygmalion*. This past summer I sat down simply to revise it and add a few more little things. I reread the book in preparation for this, and discovered that I had to throw the whole thing away and start over from scratch. Perhaps one paragraph or two pages remain intact out of that fifty pages. It also came out ninety pages long, but it's an entirely new chapter. Something had happened to my understanding of the book between three years ago and now, while other things were changing too.

HEUSSER   The sort of defacement that is necessary to reach a new understanding.

MILLER   It's a feature of reading, I think, that it allows for such change.

SCHWEIZER   I feel very much that *The Ethics of Reading* is a great change, a change of perspective.

MILLER   I suppose so. I would say two things about that. It was consciously motivated by a desire to respond to the change in literary study that was going on all around me. Part of that led to reproaches to deconstructionists for not being interested in history or politics, being apolitical, ahistorical. We spoke before about how that is an error. One way to demonstrate that, it struck me, was to write a book that faced an issue of that sort directly. I chose ethics rather than politics because I believed I could understand ethics as an arena where literature intervenes in the real world and raises questions that have to do with history and politics. The latter in their relations to literature had always seemed to me a little abstract: the notion that every time I go into the classroom I'm committing a political act. I believe that to be true, but it seems to me that it has to be mediated by a lot of steps. My turn to ethics was a way of thinking that out. But unpredictable things occurred when I started reading Kant seriously for the first time, when I read the other texts discussed in *The Ethics of Reading*, when I studied that preface to *The Golden Bowl*, for example, and asked myself what was really happening there and what I had to say about it. I would claim that the book itself is a demonstration of the argument I make in the book, namely that the beginning of the ethics of reading is the act of reading, and that that act is unpredictable, not programmable ahead of time.

HEUSSER   One of the things that occurs frequently in this context is the notion of the good reader. What exactly does this mean to you?

MILLER   It's pragmatic but also polemical. It's pragmatic in the sense that I think it is a fact. The experience that I have with students and with myself is that reading doesn't happen all that often. You can't give the same validity to every act of reading. Some people are better readers than others. Some people are better readers at some times than at others. I find the distinction between good and bad reading pragmatically valid. But the distinction is also polemical in the sense that I want to be able to say that one reading is better than another. You will not be surprised to hear me say I think Derrida is a better reader of Plato than many other scholars of Plato. The distinction also allows me to say that there are unexpected moments of what I'm calling good reading distributed somewhat unevenly here and there in the world. For example, if you read the scholarship on any work, let's say Plato's *Protagoras*, it's no surprise to find that much of it is woefully displeasing. But here and there, in the most unexpected places, you will find something that's really terrific. The most interesting thing about this is that it's not directly related to the theoretical presuppositions of the person who is doing it. You can't say: just because this person is an old-fashioned philological scholar who wrote mostly papers about Greek etymologies, he's necessarily going to write a dull and stupid paper about the *Protagoras*. It may just be the reverse. Nor can you say, just because I am equipped with the latest information about deconstruction and the new historicism and so on, that I am going to be able to produce a really good reading of something when I sit down to read it. Theory and reading are not commensurate. What I'm saying also is elitist, obviously, in that it says there are good readings and bad readings, and claims I am able to tell which ones are good and which ones are bad. So I'm getting a lot of mileage out of this distinction, and I'm willing to admit that.

HEUSSER   Does that mean that all critics should be deconstructionists?

MILLER   I'm prepared to say that all good readers *are* deconstructionists, but remember that I said there are deconstructionisms. I don't mean that everybody has to have read de Man and Derrida. What I mean is that, for me, the good readers are those readers who are, for what- ever reason, sensitive to the kinds of rhetorical complexities that Derrida, for example, sees in works. This sensitivity may be found in otherwise diverse critics. I mentioned Hölderlin as a reader of Sophocles. I think Hölderlin was a wonderful reader. He didn't have to read Derrida to be that. So, there have been a lot of good readers, and I'm prepared to say that they're all deconstructionists. But that has to be taken as a kind of jesting shorthand, yet serious. It's a shorthand for describing the sort of people who notice anomalies, who are not so bamboozled by their preconceptions about what they're going to find, that they are prepared to notice what's really strange about works. People with extremely diverse theoretical presuppositions can have this. Hegel was a good reader, even though he sometimes read only to suppress things that he didn't like, for example Friedrich Schlegel. Kierkegaard was a very good reader. He recognized what was threatening about Plato and about Socrates, and that he had somehow to put that irony down, and he also understood Hegel very well.

SCHWEIZER Is it possible that Kierkegaard is now much more appreciated because of deconstructionism?

MILLER The work is only beginning. There is the superb book by Sylviane Agacinski, which has now been translated into English, called *Aparte*. It is a wonderful book. But there is a lot more to do. I greatly regret that Paul de Man didn't live to write the Kierkegaard essay he planned. He did lecture on the book on irony and a little bit, in the seminars that I heard, on *Either/Or*.

SCHWEIZER *Fear and Trembling*, for instance, is a deconstruction of Hegel, isn't it?

MILLER Sure, but motivated, one must remember; you can't identify Kierkegaard's "deconstruction" of Hegel with Derrida's. After all, Kierkegaard was a minister, a religious writer. He recognized what's truly subversive about irony. It's a stroke of genius that he chose the concept of irony for his master's thesis. While recognizing the great danger to community, civilization, and religion in irony, the purpose of that book is to show that irony is a stage that can be surpassed. On the one hand Kierkegaard had tremendous insight into the things that made his own religious position difficult, but at the same time his commitment to that religious position is not in doubt. The difference between de Man and Kierkegaard on irony is that Kierkegaard wants to make Socrates a historical moment and irony a historical moment that can be stepped beyond, whereas for de Man, quite explicitly for example on the last page of *Allegories of Reading*, irony is the radical parabasis or suspension beyond which there is no going. De Man gets that out of Friedrich Schlegel. That's why the other presence in Kierkegaard's book on irony, also a presence in Hegel, an alien presence they recognized you had to do something against, is Friedrich Schlegel. It's the "Lucinda" Kierkegaard, like Hegel, detests. He has to dislike it, because liking it is a shorthand for admitting that the great theorist of irony in German Romanticism was Friedrich Schlegel. De Man was Schlegelian in his theory of irony. But there's more to say about this that I wish de Man had said. His jump was going to be from Kierkegaard to Marx, the Marx of *The German Ideology*. That transition would have been by way of Adorno, precisely Adorno's book on Kierkegaard, only recently now translated into English. That would have been a link to the Frankfurt School for de Man and to his thing about that, and to twentieth-century Marxist thinking about politics and literature. Somebody else ought to walk that path and try to work that sequence out.

SCHWEIZER   So Kierkegaard differs from de Man and Schlegel in advocating a possibility beyond paradox or irony.

MILLER   That's right. Kierkegaard would have said you have then to make the religious leap to the stage beyond. I may, however, be being too simplistic about de Man, who at least once said to me that religious questions are the most important ones. That doesn't mean that he gave positive answers to those questions, but it was a very clear statement and, I think, without irony on his part. It was said very solemnly and seemed to indicate that he, de Man, in his work, was also concerned with ultimate questions, meaning religious questions.

SCHWEIZER   But what about Kierkegaard's insistence that he can't make that leap? Repeatedly he distances himself from that final religious affirmation, which is impossible for anybody but, say, Abraham, or Mary.

MILLER   But he differs from de Man or Derrida or other deconstructionists in being obsessed with that impossibility. That's what he's writing about all the time.

SCHWEIZER   In that case I have always misunderstood you, and Derrida as well, because I think both of you are obsessed with that impossibility.

MILLER   I suppose, but we don't talk so much about it.

SCHWEIZER   You have talked a lot about it today.

MILLER   Yes, because you enticed me into doing so, but as I have said, it makes me uncomfortable, because it's an area where it's easy to be misunderstood.

HEUSSER   One of the precursors of these impossibilities that comes to mind is Keats's idea of negative capability. Might that be related to what you have been saying?

MILLER   Yes, that's true, though that would make Walter Jackson Bate unhappy, if he were persuaded that he had spent so much of his good time on a proto-deconstructionist. Another way in which Keats could be seen as a precursor of present-day theory would shift to something that we haven't mentioned. This seems to me of fundamental importance as a presupposition in all I've been saying about reading. It's often forgotten, in the eagerness to identify "deconstructionists" – de Man or Derrida, say, or even me – as theorists, that their work is primarily the reading of this or that or the other text. This reading is a process you could define, as Derrida does define it and I would too, as active intervention. But it also involves a patience in relationship to the text which might be defined by the negative capability, that Keatsian notion of a kind of yielding to the experience and letting happen what happens. The evidence for this in Derrida is the way the famous terms he is known for, like "dissemination", "supplement", "pharmakon", or "hymen", are not his words. They're the words of the text he happened to be reading. They're words that are ad hoc, contingent, rather than universal theoretical words. They're part of the vocabulary of the author that he's reading. They are drawn out of that author in the aid of the reading of that author. Doing that is a primary motivation of the essays in question. Often commentators abstract from de Man, Derrida, or others theoretical formulations that are stated as theory, in the sense that they have a kind of apodictic universal quality, but arise out of the act of reading some work. They have a quite different meaning when they're put back inside the essay from which they're drawn. You say, de Man says so and so, and then quote a passage out of one of his essays on Rousseau. Yes, he does say that and he meant it with the generality that's stated. But he was able to write those sentences only through the process of reading whatever passage it was that he was reading in that chapter or essay. That's often forgotten. The theoretical generalization is achieved by a kind of negative capability.

SCHWEIZER   May I ask a question about a particular passage in *The Ethics of Reading*? We were intrigued by your deliberate translation of Kant's "als so" in the second chapter. You translated that as "as if", and we were wondering how functional the questionability of that translation is? Is it a deliberate narrative or fiction on your part to exemplify an unavailable literal language? Are you exemplifying in your own language the point that you make about Kant's language?[3]

MILLER   No. That was probably just a mistake on my part, evidence of my imperfect grasp of the German language. I did my best to identify places where the translation was not quite right or missed something, and it may be a case where I simply got something wrong. I'll go back and check.[4]

There's another case in the long chapter I have written on Kleist's "The Foundling". This chapter has a section on Kant. In this case the passage is from the *First Critique*, the section on the second analogy. The second analogy is causality. The standard translation by Smith has authority. It's the one that generations of American and English students have read. The English translation subtly personifies the operation of causality, whereas Kant's phrase in German is a tautology: it happens because it happens. Kant's "Dieses geschiehet nun dadurch . . .", "Now this happens through this . . ." becomes in Smith, "This it does . . ." "It" refers to "understanding" and subtly personifies understanding, makes it an agent. In one sense the translation is a perfectly straightforward, correct translation. But by giving two different words for what in Kant are the same word, Smith makes a fundamental change. He sneaks into the notion of causality the idea that somewhere there's a shadowy person doing the causing, whereas Kant is scrupulous about the impersonality of this. He's talking not so much about causality itself as about the necessity of seeing things as caused. The point that Kant is making is that you cannot *not* see an event as caused. Seeing it as caused is a necessary part of perception, but it's not one that's motivated by anything except the fact that it happens. This example is one that I learned from Andrzej Warminski in a brilliant essay on Kleist's *Improbable Veracities*. He cites that passage and identifies the subtle difference between the German and the standard English translation, though without my emphasis on the way Smith smuggles in a personification.

HEUSSER   How does deconstruction envisage the role of the language as something that controls its creator? In other words, what was there first? After all, Daedalus was there before the labyrinth. It's not the same situation as the hen and the egg.

MILLER   I cannot speak for deconstruction, whoever she is. I imagine her, thinking of Kant's personification of the moral law, as a beautiful veiled goddess to whom I have no access. She manifests herself here and there, and as I have told you she's multifarious. She's Ms Deconstructionisms. But I can speak for myself, succinctly, in answer to your question. I do not deny that people are conscious and that language is identical neither with consciousness nor with selfhood. Putting aside areas of mute experience and mute ethical decision, if there are such things – James is a good place to think about those and worry about them – an interesting area, in some ways more controllable, is the way language, say, the language of something I read, affects my self, my consciousness, decisions and actions that I make. My feeling about these is straightforward. Reading is important because what is going to happen when I read is to some degree incalculable and unpredictable. When we put books in the hands of students, choose books for a syllabus in a course, we can't really be sure what's going to happen to this or that student when she reads such-and-such a book. Choosing a course list is a great responsibility.

Though I believe that reading may have the most momentous and decisive effects upon my selfhood and my consciousness, that does not relieve me, the I, the ego, or my consciousness, from responsibility for those effects. I think what worries people about saying that I am forced to think in a certain way by the language around me, for example what I read, is the way that it seems to lead to saying, "I can't help it, I read this book, and it turned me into a flaming revolutionary", or whatever. I would not want to say that. You have to say, "I did it, and I take responsibility for it". Though the I, the ego, is a function of language, generated, produced by language, it doesn't necessarily follow from this either that the "I" doesn't exist, or that sentences that take the form of "I must do so and so", or "I choose so and so", or "I accept a responsibility for so and so", don't make sense.

What I've been saying leads to the question of performative language. As Gasché and others have observed, the traditional analysis of performative speech acts, say in Austin, depends on the concept of the "I". The exemplary performatives involve the word "I". "I pronounce you man and wife." "I promise to do so and so." "I bet so and so." "I excuse myself from doing . . ." "I'm sorry I did it." "I didn't mean to do it." "I christen thee the Queen Mary." The "I" is always there, though sometimes only implicitly. The efficacy of performative speech acts presupposes the "I", the willing, choosing, conscious "I" acting with the proper authority and in the proper circumstances. The deconstructive analysis of speech acts, for example by de Man or Derrida, has put the authority of that intending "I" in question, but not by saying you should not hold somebody responsible for the effects of speech acts they utter. When I say, "I promise to do so and so", as Hyacinth did when he promised to act in a certain way for the revolutionaries in James' *The Princess Casamassima*, the promise is binding. He must keep it or break it. But the "I" does not, cannot, wholly control or predict the effect the speech act is going to have. The double bind or the awkwardness of performatives is the following: On the one hand you must say, "I did it, I made this promise", or "I declared this congress open and begun", "I did it and must take responsibility for it". At the same time that does not mean, as Austin would wish, you can predict what's going to happen. Something is going to happen. The speech act acts. It's going to be efficacious, and you're not going to be relieved of responsibility for that effect. But it is not necessarily going to be what you wish would happen. It's a little as though, when you say, "I pronounce you man and wife", the result were to be something entirely different, not a divorce necessarily, but some other result from the one intended.

On the question of muteness and silence, I have only begun to think about that. In James's novels, for example, it's not just that there are things that are not represented, like sex, the moment of promise, and the moment of death, but that James's novels are full of communications and, I think you would have to say, something like speech acts, that are not spoken at all, that are nowhere verbalized, neither by the narrator nor by the character himself or herself. Or they are verbalized only in non-significant pieces of language like exclamations. Or they exist as the lifting of an eyebrow or the raising of a hand. These function like language, but language of a very peculiar kind, function in both ways, both in conveying knowledge and in functioning like speech acts. James seems to have been interested in such non-verbal signs. I was thinking earlier that one could write a wonderful essay on "Oh!" in *The Wings of the Dove*. It appears over and over – I have only just now noticed it. "Oh!" is in one place thematized, called to the reader's attention. Densher admires Lord Mark, who's the real aristocrat, whereas Densher is just an American journalist, for his mastery of the "Oh". Lord Mark is introduced to Densher, and he says, "Oh". James then talks about the way in which an infinite amount is conveyed in this "Oh". When I saw that, I began to notice that Densher and others pick up the "Oh!" There are moments in the novel when a character simply says, "Oh". The "Oh" carries a tremendous burden, both of information conveyed from one character to another, and of efficacious performance. Kate, on the very last page of the novel, says (I paraphrase from memory), "If you tell me you are not in love with her memory (the memory of Milly Theale), I will give up the money and marry you". Densher has conveyed to Kate, she guesses it because he never actually says it, that he'll marry her only if she gives up the money. Densher, you'll remember, makes all the money over to Kate that he's got from Milly. He says he's going to do this, and she says, "This means you'll marry me without the money, with the money you won't", and he says, "Yes". Her next move – it's like a complicated chess game – is to say, "I will marry you if you will assure me you're not in love with Milly Theale's memory". His answer is, "Oh, her memory". That's the last of those "Oh's". This last "Oh" conveys a lot. It's certainly not a normal speech act, which would require an articulated sentence, at least something minimal like "I do". It's certainly not a normal piece of constative language either. It's not really language at all. It's an exclamation, an inarticulate cry, without referential or syntactic sense. Nevertheless it bears a tremendous weight. Thinking through the relation between consciousness and the self, on the one hand, and language, on the other, might have to include some analysis of kinds of language that are not really language in the usual sense. For James, and probably in most usage, such cries support neither the sort of protest we make when we say, "Of course there's consciousness without language, you cannot tell me that language entirely produces consciousness because I know otherwise", nor on the other hand, the answer to that, that says "No, no, without language, no consciousness". Here's an in-between thing that is language and not language. James was a master of its uses, the master of the "Oh!"

SCHWEIZER   What will be the future of deconstruction?

MILLER   I answer in Matthew Arnold's words. He says the future of poetry is immense, and I say the future of deconstruction is immense, and then qualify that by saying, who knows? I add two things that are not so much prophecies as descriptions of present fact. One: one of the things you get out of saying "deconstructionisms" – in the plural – is to recognize that "deconstruction" becomes transformed into whatever people make it into. For example, one definition of deconstruction is quite false to the work of actual people in the field. I mean the definition of it given by the mass media in recent attacks on de Man and elsewhere.[5] There is now a so-called "deconstruction" defined as nihilism, as saying it's all language, and that language is all the free play of words in the void, as saying you can make language mean anything you want, as ahistorical and aestheticist. An interesting mistake, because part of that misidentification equates deconstruction with reader-response criticism, a very different thing. All those generalizations are demonstrably in error. Nevertheless among the other deconstructions is a false ideological construct made up by Jon Wiener, Walter Kendrick, the author of the piece in *Newsweek*, and others. Since a lot of people believe that's what deconstruction is, this fabrication therefore has existence in the world, political existence. There are also many happier versions of deconstruction that differ quite a bit from one another. It's by no means possible to reconcile Derrida and de Man completely, or the work of those two with my own work, and that's good to remember. That's the first point.

The second point would be to say that it's also quite clear that deconstructionisms have gone into another mode of influence. They have begun to be widely assimilated, and transformed in two ways: one, in other disciplines, and, secondly, in other countries. Assimilate and transform – one has to hold onto both of those. "Deconstructionisms" are influential in architectural theory, in people like Peter Eisenmann, Bernard Tschumi, other architects who read Derrida, even read me. That has had a decisive effect not only on their architectural theory but even on the buildings that they design. I think that was less predictable than the more expected influences – in theology, in legal theory, now in philosophy, and in other disciplines. The word "influence" is probably not the right word. "Effect" or "action" might be better. So-called critical legal theory is deeply influenced by what it understands of deconstruction and of reader-response criticism.

The resistances to this kind of critical theory are different in the different disciplines. In theology, for example, the things that cause so much hostility and resistance to deconstructionisms in literary study don't seem to trouble biblical scholars as much. For example, the notion of a certain contradictory indetermination in the meaning of a given text. They say, well, that's something we're prepared to accept about biblical texts. It's not that such notions are not controversial and vigorously so within biblical studies, but that the field of the discipline it enters is quite different. The same thing may be said for philosophy. There's tremendous resistance to Derrida, as you know, in American philosophy. They say he's not a philospher at all, and so on. Nevertheless, bit by bit, deconstructionisms are beginning to have an effect on American philosophy. That effect will have its own contours and directions.

The same thing may be said about the working of deconstructionisms in other countries. I've lectured in Japan and China; I'm going off to Moscow in June of 1990; I've been in Uruguay, Argentina, and Spain. I discover wherever I go that this work is known, is being read and translated. But what is happening is not just assimilation but transformation. Who knows what the People's Republic of China is going to make out of Western literary theory? I'm involved as co-editor of a translation project with a scholar at the Chinese Academy of Social Sciences in Beijing, Fengzhen Wang. Wang is the chief person there charged with writing books and essays about Western literary theory, and then seeing that it is translated. Wang and I are engaged in preparing what may be as many as fifty volumes of translations of ten essays each by Western theorists. Not just deconstructionists. The project will include all the major "deconstructionists", but also Jameson, Iser, Fish, Poulet, etc. What will be the effect of that in China is incalculable. Something will happen.

So deconstructionisms have now been widely diffused. They will be assimilated and transformed, even by modes of literary theory that are, at least superficially, strongly opposed, for example, new historicism. The relationship between what the new historicists are doing and what deconstruction did a little bit earlier is paradoxical. The new historicists say, "Deconstructionists didn't do what we are doing. They had no interest in history and politics. We're now going to redress that balance". At the same time many theoretical presuppositions of the new historicism come directly from deconstruction. It's not that it's not different, but the work of the new historicists would be impossible without the intervening period of deconstruction, even though they spend a lot of time attacking us for one reason or another. It's not simply in bad faith or as a kind of denegation. They are very conscious of the ways they are different. No doubt there's little in the work of the deconstructionists of the archival historical research I was praising in the new historicists, but reflection about history is by no means absent in de Man or Derrida. The new historicism would be impossible without deconstructionisms.

I'm not a prophet, but I think that the episode called deconstruction in literary study, philosophy, and cultural critique is not only a permanent part of history now, but is still productive and active, and will go on being so. That's one of the things that annoys people. It has occurred, and it is now unstoppable. I don't know how Derrida thinks of himself, but you and I can look at Derrida's work and see that he is someone who will be, like Foucault, a permanent part of the history of Western thought. He has abundance, originality, brilliance, force. He will go on being read. Two hundred years from now, he will still be there, in the same way that Fichte and Hegel are.

HEUSSER Or Nietzsche.

MILLER Or Nietzsche, that's right.

NOTES

1   "It is the ending which has to be protected as it were against the beginning." (Friedrich Hölderlin, "Remarks on 'Oedipus'"; *Essays and Letters on Theory*, trans. Thomas Pfau (Albany: State University of New York Press, 1988) p. 102.) Here, from the same translation, is Hölderlin's definition of the break in the tragic action he calls "transport" or "caesura":

> For indeed, the tragic *transport* is actually empty and the least restrained.
>
> Thereby, in the rhythmic sequence of the representations wherein *transport* presents itself, there becomes necessary *what in poetic meter is called caesura*, the pure word, the counter-rhythmic rupture; namely, in order to meet the onrushing change of representations at its highest point in such a manner that very soon there does not appear the change of representation but the representation itself. (ibid., pp. 101–2)

Hölderlin explains as follows why the speeches of Teiresias form the caesuras of both plays: "He enters the course of fate as the custodian of the natural power which, in a tragic manner, removes man from his own life-sphere, the center of his inner life into another world and into the eccentric sphere of the dead" (ibid., p. 102).

2   *PMLA* 102, no. 3 (May 1987).

3   This question is taken up in the second section of the Introduction.

4   The paperback edition of *The Ethics of Reading* now corrects this error, with the help of consultation with Martin Heusser. My reading of this section of Kant's *Grundlegung* remains essentially the same. It was not dependent on mistranslating "als so" as "as if" rather than "in such a manner" (JHM: 8/15/89).

5   I have expressed my judgement of the relation between de Man's later work and the recently discovered wartime writings in two essays, "NB", *TLS*, 17–23 June, 1988, pp. 676, 685, and "An Open Letter to Professor Jon Wiener", *Responses on Paul de Man's Wartime Journalism* (Lincoln, Nebraska: University of Nebraska Press, 1989) pp. 334–42.

J. Hillis Miller: *A Bibliography,* 1955–1990

1955

1 "The Creation of the Self in Gerard Manley Hopkins", *ELH* 22, no. 1 (March) pp. 293–319.

1957

2 "Franz Kafka and the Metaphysics of Alienation", in Scott Jr., Nathan A. (ed.), *The Tragic Vision and the Christian Faith* (New York: Association Press) pp. 281–305.

1958

3 *Charles Dickens: The World of His Novels* (Cambridge: Harvard University Press; Bloomington: Indiana University Press) 346 pp.; reissued 1968 (Cambridge: Harvard University Press); 1969 (Bloomington: Indiana University Press). First Midland Book Edition.

4 "Oliver Twist", in *Charles Dickens: The World of His Novels* (Cambridge: Harvard University Press), pp. 36–84. Reprinted as "The Dark World of *Oliver Twist*", in Bloom, Harold (ed.), *Charles Dickens*, Modern Critical Views (New York: Chelsea House Publishers, 1987) pp. 29–69.

1960

5   "The Anonymous Walkers", *Nation* 190, no. 17 (April) pp. 351–4.

1961

6   "'Orion' in 'The Wreck of the Deutschland'", *Modern Language Notes* 76, no. 6 (June) pp. 509–14.

1962

7   (With George Ford, Edgar Johnson, Sylvère Monod, and Noel Peyrouton), *Dickens Criticism: Past, Present, and Future Directions* (Cambridge: The Charles Dickens Reference Center) 64 pp.
8   Introduction, *Oliver Twist* by Charles Dickens (New York: Holt, Rinehart, and Winston).

1963

9   *The Disappearance of God: Five Nineteenth-Century Writers* (Cambridge: Belknap Press of Harvard University Press) ix, 367 pp.; reissued 1965 (New York: Schocken Books); 1975 (Cambridge: Belknap Press of Harvard University Press).
10   "The Literary Criticism of George Poulet", *Modern Language Notes* 78, no. 5 (December) pp. 471–88. Reprinted in *Mercure de France*, 1965, pp. 652–74 as "La Critique de Georges Poulet". Reprinted in Hardison Jr., O.B. (ed.), *The Quest for Imagination* (Cleveland: The Press of Case Western Reserve University, 1971) pp. 191–205.
11   "The Theme of the Disappearance of God in Victorian Poetry", *Victorian Studies* 6, no. 3 (March) pp. 207–27.

1964

12   Afterword, *Our Mutual Friend* by Charles Dickens (New York: New American Library) pp. 901–11.
13   "Wallace Stevens's Poetry of Being", *ELH* 31, no. 1 (March) pp. 86–105.

1965

14   (Ed. with Roy Harvey Pearce), *The Act of the Mind: Essays on the Poetry of Wallace Stevens* (Baltimore: Johns Hopkins University Press) xi, 287 pp.
15   *Poets of Reality: Six Twentieth-Century Writers* (Cambridge: Belknap Press of Harvard University Press; New York: Atheneum) 369 pp.; reissued 1966, 1984 (Cambridge: Belknap Press of Harvard University Press); 1969, 1974 (New York: Atheneum).

1966

16   (Edited with an introduction), *William Carlos Williams: A Collection of Critical Essays*, Twentieth Century Views (Englewood Cliffs: Prentice-Hall) viii, 182 pp.
17   "The Antitheses of Criticism: Reflections on the Yale Colloquium", *Modern Language Notes* 81, no. 5, pp. 557–71.
18   "The Geneva School: The Criticism of Marcel Raymond, Albert Béguin, Georges Poulet, Jean Rousset, Jean-Pierre Richard, and Jean Starobinski", *Critical Quarterly* 8, no. 4 (Winter) pp. 302–21. Reprinted in *Virginia Quarterly Review* 43, no. 3 (Summer 1967) pp. 465–88; trans. into Spanish in *Asomante* 24 (Abril–Junio 1968) pp. 7–23; and reprinted in Simon, John K. (ed.), *Modern French Criticism* (Chicago: University of Chicago Press, 1970) pp. 277–310.
19   "Some Implications of Form in Victorian Fiction", *Comparative Literature Studies* 3, no. 2, pp. 109–18. Reprinted in Panichas, George A. (ed.), *Mansions of the Spirit: Essays in Religion and Literature* (New York: Hawthorn Books, 1967) pp. 200–12.

1967

20 "Charles Dickens", in *The New Catholic Encyclopedia* 4 (New York: McGraw-Hill) pp. 856–7.

21 "Literature and Religion" in Thorpe, James Ernest (ed.), *Relations of Literary Study: Essays on Interdisciplinary Contributions* (New York: Modern Language Association) pp. 111–26. Reprinted and translated into German in *Interdisziplinäre Perspektiven der Literatur* (Stuttgart: Ferdinand Enke, 1977) pp. 132–50.

22 "Thomas Hardy: A Sketch for a Portrait", in *De Ronsard à Breton: Hommages à Marcel Raymond* (Paris: Corti) pp. 195–206.

23 "Recent Work on Hardy", *Victorian Studies* 10, no. 3 (March) pp. 278–82 (Roy Morrell, Harold Orel, Benjamin Sankey and Carl Weber).

1968

24 *The Form of Victorian Fiction: Thackeray, Dickens, Trollope, George Eliot, Meredith and Hardy* (Notre Dame: University of Notre Dame Press) xiii, 151 pp.; Second Edition with a new preface (Cleveland: Arete Press, 1979).

25 "Three Problems of Fictional Form: First Person Narration in *David Copperfield* and *Huckleberry Finn*", in Pearce, Roy Harvey (ed.), *Experience in the Novel* (New York: Columbia University Press) pp. 21–48.

26 "'Wessex Heights': The Persistence of the Past in Hardy's Poetry", *Critical Quarterly* 10, no. 4 (Winter) pp. 339–59. Reprinted in an expanded version as "History as Repetition in Thomas Hardy's Poetry: The Example of 'Wessex Heights'", in Bradbury, M. and Palmer, D. (eds), *Victorian Poetry*, Stratford-upon-Avon Studies (London: Edward Arnold, 1972) pp. 222–53.

27 "William Carlos Williams: The Doctor as Poet", *Plexus* 3, no. 4 (June) pp. 19–20.

1969

28   "I'd Have My Life Unbe: La Ricerca dell'obblio nell'opera di Thomas Hardy", *Strumenti Critici* 3, pp. 263–85.

29   "Howe on Hardy's Art", *Novel* 2, no. 3 (Spring) pp. 272–77 (Review of Kronenberger, Louis (ed.), *Thomas Hardy* by Irving Howe).

30   "Recent Studies in the Nineteenth Century", *Studies in English Literature 1500–1900* 9, no. 4 (Autumn) pp. 737–53; vol. 10, no. 1 (Winter, 1970) pp. 183–214 (Review of books on nineteenth-century literature published between Sept. 1968 and Sept. 1969).

1970

31   *Thomas Hardy: Distance and Desire* (Cambridge: Belknap Press of Harvard University Press) xvi, 282 pp.

32   "Geneva or Paris: The Recent Work of Georges Poulet", *University of Toronto Quarterly* 39, no. 3 (April) pp. 212–28. Reprinted in Hardison Jr., O.B. (ed.), *The Quest for Imagination* (Cleveland: The Press of Case Western Reserve University, 1971) pp. 205–24.

33   "The Interpretation of *Lord Jim*" in Bloomfield, Morton W. (ed.), *The Interpretation of Narrative: Theory and Practice*, Harvard English Studies 1 (Cambridge: Harvard University Press) pp. 211–28.

34   "The Sources of Dickens's Comic Art: From *American Notes* to *Martin Chuzzlewit*", *Nineteenth-Century Fiction*, 24, no. 4 (March) pp. 467–76.

35   "Virginia Woolf's All Souls' Day: The Omniscient Narrator in *Mrs Dalloway*", in Friedman, Melvin J. and Vickery, John B. (eds), *The Shaken Realist: Essays in Modern Literature in Honor of Frederick J. Hoffman* (Baton Rouge: Louisiana State University Press) pp. 100–27.

36   "Williams' *Spring and All* and the Progress of Poetry", *Daedalus* 99, no. 1 (Winter) pp. 405–34.

1971

37 (Ed. with a Foreword), *Aspects of Narrative: Selected Papers from the English Institute* (New York: Columbia University Press) x, 210 pp.

38 "The Fiction of Realism: *Sketches by Boz, Oliver Twist*, and Cruikshank's Illustrations", in *Charles Dickens and George Cruickshank* by J. Hillis Miller and David Borowitz (Los Angeles: Williams Andrews Clark Memorial Library, University of California) pp. 1–69. Reprinted in Nisbet, Ada and Nevius, Blake (eds), *Dickens's Centennial Essays* (Berkeley: University of California Press) pp. 85–153.

39 "Georges Poulet's 'Criticism of Identification'", in Hardison, Jr., O. B. (ed.), *The Quest for Imagination: Essays in Twentieth-Century Aesthetic Criticism* (Cleveland: The Press of Case Western Reserve University) pp. 191–224.

40 Introduction, in Page, Norman (ed.), *Bleak House* by Charles Dickens, (Harmondsworth: Penguin Books) pp. 11–34.

41 "The Still Heart: Poetic Form in Wordsworth", *New Literary History* 2, no. 2 (Winter) pp. 297–310.

1972

42 "Tradition and Difference", *diacritics* 2, no. 4 (Winter) pp. 6–13 (Review of *Natural Supernaturalism* by M. H. Abrams).

1973

43 "The Stone and the Shell: The Problem of Poetic Form in Wordsworth's 'Dream of the Arab'" in *Mouvements premiers: Études critiques offertes à Georges Poulet* (Paris: Corti) pp. 125–47.

1974

44 "Narrative and History", *ELH* 41, no. 3 (Fall) pp. 455–73. Reprinted and trans. into Polish, *Pamietnik Literacki* 75, no. 3, 1984, pp. 301–17.

1975

45 "Fiction and Repetition: *Tess of the d'Urbervilles*" in Friedman, Allen Warren (ed.), *Forms of British Fiction* (Austin: University of Texas Press) pp. 43–71.

46 Introduction, *The Well-Beloved: A Sketch of Temperament* by Thomas Hardy, The New Wessex Edition (London: Macmillan) pp. 11–21.

47 "Myth as "Hieroglyph" in Ruskin", *Studies in the Literary Imagination* 8, no. 2 (Fall) pp. 15–18.

48 "Optic and Semiotic in *Middlemarch*", in Buckley, Jerome H. (ed.), *The Worlds of Victorian Fiction*, Harvard English Studies 6 (Cambridge: Harvard University Press) pp. 125–45.

49 "A Panel Discussion" (with James Cowan, James Gindin, Charles Rossman, and Avrom Fleishman), in Friedman, Alan Warren (ed.), *Forms of Modern British Fiction* (Austin: University of Texas Press) pp. 201–32.

50 "Deconstructing the Deconstructors", *diacritics* 5, no. 2 (Summer) pp. 24–31 (Review of *The Inverted Bell* by Joseph N. Riddel).

51 "The Year's Books: J. Hillis Miller on Literary Criticism", *New Republic* 173, no. 22, 29 November, pp. 30–3.

1976

52 "Ariadne's Thread: Repetition and the Narrative Line", *Critical Inquiry* 3, no. 1 (Autumn) pp. 57–77. Reprinted in Valdes, Mario J. and Miller, Owen (eds), *Interpretation of Narrative* (Toronto: University of Toronto Press, 1978) pp. 148–66.

53 "The Linguistic Moment in 'The Wreck of the Deutsch-
    land'", in Young, Thomas D. (ed.), *The New Criticism and
    After* (Charlottesville: University Press of Virginia)
    pp. 47–60.

54 "Stevens' Rock and Criticism as Cure", *Georgia Review* 30,
    nos. 1–2, (Spring/Summer) pp. 5–31, 330–48. Reprinted in
    Bloom, Harold (ed.), *Wallace Stevens*, Modern Critical
    Views (New York: Chelsea House Publishers, 1985)
    pp. 27–49. Second half reprinted as "Stevens' Rock and
    Criticism as Cure, II", in Davis, Robert Con (ed.), *Contem-
    porary Literary Criticism* (New York: Longman, 1986)
    pp. 416–27.

55 "Walter Pater: A Partial Portrait", *Daedalus* 105, no. 1
    (Winter) pp. 97–113. Reprinted in Bloom, Harold (ed.),
    Walter Pater, Modern Critical Views (New York: Chelsea
    House Publishers, 1985) pp. 75–95.

56 "Beginning with a Text", *diacritics* 6, no. 3 (Fall) pp. 2–7
    (Review of *Beginnings* by Edward W. Said).

1977

57 "Ariachne's Broken Woof", *Georgia Review* 31, no. 1
    (Spring) pp. 44–60.

58 "The Critic as Host", *Critical Inquiry* 3, no. 3 (Spring
    pp. 439–47. Reprinted in Bloom, Harold et al. (ed.), *Decon-
    struction and Criticism* (New York: The Seabury Press, 1979)
    pp. 217–253; in Adams, Hazard and Searle, Leroy (eds),
    Critical Theory Since 1965 (Tallahassee: Florida State Univer-
    sity Press, 1986) pp. 452–468, and in *Pamietnik Literacki*
    77, no. 2 (1986) pp. 285–95. Reprinted as "El Critico como
    huesped, J. Hillis Miller", trans. Barbara Trotsko and Man-
    uel Alcides Jofre, in Blanco, Monica and Jofre, Manuel
    Alcides (eds), *Para leer al lector* (Santiago: Universidad
    Metropolitana de Ciencias de la Educacion, 1987)
    pp. 223–55.

59 "Nature and the Linguistic Moment", in Knoepflmacher,
    U. C. and Tennyson, G. B. (eds), *Nature and the Victorian
    Imagination* (Berkeley: University of California Press)
    pp. 440–51.

1978

60   "Narrative Middles: A Preliminary Outline", *Genre* 11, no. 3 (Fall) pp. 375–87.
61   "The Problematic of Ending in Narrative", *Narrative Endings, Nineteenth-Century Fiction* (Special Issue) 33, no. 1 (June) pp. 3–7.
62   Review of *The Novels of Anthony Trollope* by J. R. Kincaid, *Yale Review*, 67, no. 2, pp. 276–9.

1979

63   "Béguin, Balzac, Trollope et la Double Analogie Redoublée", trans. Georges Poulet, *Albert Béguin et Marcel Raymond*, Colloque de Cartigny (Paris: Corti) pp. 135–54.
64   "A 'Buchstäbliches' Reading of *The Elective Affinities*", *Glyph* 6, pp. 1–23.
65   "The Function of Rhetorical Study at the Present Time", *The State of the Discipline: 1970s–1980s, ADE Bulletin* (Special Issue) no. 62 (September/November) pp. 10–18.
66   "Kenneth Burke", in Sills, David L. (ed.), *International Encyclopedia of the Social Sciences: Biographical Supplement 18* (New York: The Free Press; London: Macmillan) pp. 78–81.
67   "On Edge: The Crossways of Contemporary Criticism", *Bulletin of the American Academy of Arts and Sciences* 32, no. 4 (January) pp. 13–32. Reprinted in Eaves, Morris and Fischer, Michael (eds.) *Romanticism and Contemporary Criticism* (Ithaca: Cornell University Press, 1986) pp. 96–126.
68   "Theology and Logology in Victorian Literature", *Journal of the American Academy of Religion* 47, no. 2 (Supplement) pp. 345–61.
69   Review of *Triptych and the Cross: Central Myths of George Eliot's Poetic Imagination* by F. Bonaparte, *Notre Dame English Journal* 12, no. 1 pp. 78–80.

1980

70 "The Figure in the Carpet", *Poetics Today* 1, no. 3 (Spring) pp. 107–18.

71 "A Guest in the House: Reply to Shlomith Rimmon-Kenan's Reply", *Poetics Today* 2, no. 1 (Winter, 1980–81) pp. 189–91.

72 With others: "*Middlemarch*, Chapter 85: Three Commentaries", *Nineteenth-Century Fiction* 35, no. 3 (December) pp. 432–53.

73 "The Rewording Shell: Natural Image and Symbolic Emblem in Yeats's Early Poetry", in Hagenbüchle, Roland and Swann, Joseph T. (eds), *Poetic Knowledge: Circumference and Center* (Bonn: Bouvier) pp. 75–86.

74 "Theoretical and Atheoretical in Stevens", in Doggett, Frank and Buttel, Robert (eds), *Wallace Stevens: A Celebration* (Princeton: Princeton University Press) pp. 274–85.

75 "Theory and Practice: Response to Vincent Leitch", *Critical Inquiry* 6, no. 4 (Summer) pp. 609–14.

76 "*Wuthering Heights* and the Ellipses of Interpretation", *Notre Dame English Journal* 12, no. 2 (April) pp. 85–100.

77 "Master Mariner of the Imagination", *Washington Post*, Book World Section 10, no. 14, 6 April, pp. 1, 8 (Review of *Conrad in the Nineteenth Century* by Ian Watt).

1981

78 "Character in the Novel: A Real Illusion", in Mintz, Samuel; Chandler, Alice; and Mulvey, Christopher (eds), *From Smollett to James: Studies in the Novel and Other Essays Presented to Edgar Johnson* (Charlottesville: University Press of Virginia) pp. 277–85.

79 "The Disarticulation of the Self in Nietzsche", *Monist* 64, no. 2 (April) pp. 247–61.

80 "Dismembering and Disremembering in Nietzsche's 'On Truth and Lies in a Non-Moral Sense'", *Boundary 2* 9, no. 3 (Spring/Fall) pp. 41–54. Reprinted in O'Hara, Daniel (ed.),

Why Nietzsche Now? (Bloomington: Indiana University Press, 1985) pp. 41–54.

81   "The Ethics of Reading: Vast Gaps and Parting Hours", in Konigsberg, Ira (ed.), *American Criticism in the Poststructuralist Age*, Michigan Studies in the Humanities (Ann Arbor: University of Michigan Press) pp. 19–41.

82   Introduction, Hall, John N. (ed.), *Cousin Henry* by Anthony Trollope (New York: Arno Press) pp. v–xiii.

83   Introduction, Hall, John N. (ed.), *Lady Anna* by Anthony Trollope (New York: Arno Press).

84   "Topography in *The Return of the Native, Essays in Literature* 8, no. 2 (Fall) pp. 119–34.

85   "The Two Allegories", in Bloomfield, Morton W. (ed.), *Allegory, Myth and Symbol*, Harvard English Studies 9 (Cambridge: Harvard University Press) pp. 355–70.

86   Review of *Celestial Pantomine* by Justus George Lawler, *Commonweal* 108, no. 19 (23 October) pp. 601–4.

1982

87   *Fiction and Repetition: Seven English Novels* (Cambridge: Harvard University Press; Oxford: Blackwell) vi, 250 pp.

88   "From Narrative Theory to Joyce; From Joyce to Narrative Theory", in Benstock, Bernard (ed.), *The Seventh of Joyce* (Bloomington: Indiana University Press; Sussex, England: The Harvester Press) pp. 3–4.

89   "Parable and Performative in the Gospels and in Modern Literature", in Tucker, Gene M. and Knight, Douglas A. (eds), *Humanizing America's Iconic Book* (Chico, CA: Scholar's Press), pp. 57–71.

90   "La Señora Dalloway: La repetición como resurrección de los muertos", *La Desconstrucción: Los criticos de Yale*, Comisión Fulbright (Diciembre, 1985) pp. 13–21, from *Fiction and Repetition*, pp. 176–202.

91   "Tribute to Georges Poulet" (with Richard Macksey, Paul de Man, George Armstrong Kelly and Jean Starobinski), *Modern Language Notes* 97, no. 5 (December) pp. v–xii.

92   "Trollope's Thackeray", *Nineteenth-Century Literature* 37, no. 3 (December) pp. 350–7.

93 Review of *The Interpretation of Otherness: Literature, Religion, and the American Imagination* by Giles Gunn, *Journal of Religion* 62, no. 3 (July) pp. 299–304.

1983

94 "'Herself Against Herself': The Clarification of Clara Middleton", in Heilbrun, Carolyn G. and Higonnet, Margaret R. (eds), *The Representation of Women in Fiction* (Baltimore: The Johns Hopkins University Press) pp. 98–123.
95 "Mr Carmichael and Lily Briscoe: The Rhythm of Creativity in *To the Lighthouse*", in Kiely, Robert and Hildebidle, John (eds), *Modernism Reconsidered* (Cambridge: Harvard University Press) pp. 167–89.
96 "The Two Relativisms: Point of View and Indeterminacy in the Novel: *Absalom, Absalom!*", in Craige, Betty Jean (ed.), *Relativism in the Arts* (Athens: The University of Georgia Press) pp. 148–70.

1984

97 "Constructions in Criticism", *Boundary 2* 12, no. 3/13, no. 1 (Spring/Fall) pp. 157–72.
98 Introduction, "Interview with Paul de Man" by Robert Moynihan, *Yale Review* 73, no. 4 (Summer) pp. 576–602.
99 (With B. Johnson and L. Mackey), "Marxism and Deconstruction", *Genre* 17, nos. 1–2, pp. 75–97. Reprinted in Davis, Robert Con and Schleifer, Ronald (eds), *Rhetoric and Form: Deconstruction at Yale* (Norman: University of Oklahoma Press, 1985) pp. 75–97.
100 "The Search for Grounds in Literary Study", *Genre* 17, nos. 1–2 (Spring/Summer) pp. 19–36. Reprinted in Davis, Robert Con and Schleifer, Ronald (eds), *Rhetoric and Form: Deconstruction at Yale* (Norman: University of Oklahoma Press, 1985) pp. 19–36; in Davis, Robert Con and Schleifer, Ronald (eds), *Contemporary Literary Criticism, Second*

Edition (New York: Longman, 1989) pp. 566–78; and in Davis, Robert Con, and Finke, Laurie (eds), *Literary Criticism and Theory: The Greeks to the Present* (New York: Longman, 1989) pp. 814–27.

101   "Thomas Hardy, Jacques Derrida, and the 'Dislocation of Souls'", in Smith, Joseph H. and Kerrigan, William (eds), *Taking Chances: Derrida, Psychoanalysis and Literature* (Baltimore: The Johns Hopkins University Press), pp. 31–50.

1985

102   *The Linguistic Moment: From Wordsworth to Stevens* (Princeton: Princeton University Press) xxi, 445 pp.; reissued 1987.

103   "Gleichnis in Nietzsche's 'Also Sprach Zarathustra'", *International Studies in Philosophy* 17, no. 2, pp. 3–15.

104   "*Heart of Darkness* Revisited", in Murfin Ross C. (ed.), *Conrad Revisited: Essays for the Eighties* (University: University of Alabama Press) pp. 31–50.

105   "Impossible Metaphor: Wallace Stevens's 'The Red Fern' as Example", in Brooks, Peter; Felman, Shoshana; and Miller, J. Hillis (eds), *The Lesson of Paul de Man, Yale French Studies* (Special Issue) no. 69, pp. 150–62.

106   "The Linguistic Moment", in Bloom, Harold (ed.), *Gerard Manley Hopkins*, Modern Critical Views (New York: Chelsea House Publishers, 1986) pp. 147–62.

107   "In Memoriam" in Brooks, Peter; Felman, Shoshana; and Miller, J. Hillis (eds), *The Lesson of Paul de Man, Yale French Studies* (Special Issue) no. 69, pp. 3–4.

108   "Topography and Tropography in Thomas Hardy's *In Front of the Landscape*", in Valdes, Mario J. and Miller, Owen (eds), *Identity of the Literary Text* (Toronto: University of Toronto Press), pp. 73–91. Reprinted in Machin, Richard and Norris, Christopher (eds) *Post-Structuralist Readings of English Poetry* (Cambridge: Cambridge University Press, 1987) pp. 332–48.

109   "The Two Rhetorics: George Eliot's Bestiary", in Atkins, G. Douglas and Johnson, Michael L. (eds), *Writing and*

Reading Differently: Deconstruction and the Teaching of Composition and Literature (Lawrence: University Press of Kansas) pp. 101–14.

1986

110 "Catachresis, Prosopopoeia, and the Pathetic Fallacy: The Rhetoric of Ruskin" in Hagenbüchle, Roland and Skandera, Laura (eds), *Poetry and Epistemology: Turning Points in the History of Poetic Knowledge* (Regensburg: Verlag Friedrich Pustet) pp. 398–407.

111 "The Future for the Study of Languages and Literatures", *MLA Newsletter* 18, no. 4 (Winter) pp. 3–4.

112 "How Deconstruction Works", *New York Times Magazine*, 9 February, p. 25.

113 "Is There an Ethics of Reading?", a lecture delivered at the 58th general meeting of the English Literary Society of Japan (Tokyo: English Literary Society) pp. 2–25. Reprinted and trans. into Spanish by Raquel Garcia de Sanjurjo as "Existe una Etica de la Lectura?", *La Deconstrucción: Otro Descubrimiento de America*, Diseminario (Montevideo, Uruguay: XYZ Editores, 1987) pp. 197–226.

114 "The Obligation to Write", *MLA Newsletter* 18, no. 3 (Fall) pp. 4–5.

115 "Responsibility and the Joy of Reading", *MLA Newsletter* 18, no. 1 (Spring) p. 2.

116 "Responsibility and the Joy (?) of Teaching", *MLA Newsletter* 18, no. 2 (Summer) p. 2.

117 "When is a Primitive Like an Orb?" in Caws, Mary Ann (ed.), *Textual Analysis: Some Readers Reading* (New York: Modern Language Association) pp. 167–81.

1987

118 *The Ethics of Reading: Kant, de Man, Eliot, Trollope, James and Benjamin* (The Wellek Library Lectures at University of California, Irvine) (New York: Columbia University Press) xi, 138 pp.

119   "L'Apocalisse Non è Mai Ora", trans. Liliana Cioppettini, *In Forma Di Parole* (Ottobre, Novembre, Diciembre) pp. 25–36.

120   "Deconstruction in Japan? A letter to Professor Taketoshi Furomoto", *Japanese translation in Kobe*, Japanese newspaper (February).

121   "The Ethics of Reading", *Style* 21, no. 2 (Summer) pp. 181–91.

122   "Figure in Borges's 'Death and the Compass': Red Scharlach as Hermeneut", *Dieciocho* 10, no. 1 (Spring) pp. 53–62. Reprinted and trans. Maria Ines Segundo as "La Figura en 'La Muerte y la Brujula' de Borges: Red Scharlach como Hermeneuta", in Block de Behar, Lisa (ed.) *La Desconstrucción: Otro Descubrimiento de America*, Diseminario (Montevideo, Uruguay: XYZ Editores) pp. 163–73.

123   "The Imperative to Teach", *Qui Parle* 1, no. 2 (Spring) pp. 1–7.

124   "Lectura de Escritura: George Eliot", trans. Laura Flores, *La Desconstrucción: Otro Descubrimiento de America*, Diseminario (Montevideo, Uruguay: XYZ Editores) pp. 175–96.

125   "Presidential Address 1986: The Triumph of Theory, the Resistance to Reading, and the Question of the Material Base", *PMLA* 102, no. 3 (May) pp. 281–91.

126   (With D. A. Miller) "The Profession of English: An Exchange", *ADE Bulletin*, no. 88 (Winter) pp. 42–58.

127   "William Carlos Williams and Wallace Stevens", in Elliott, Emory et al. (eds), *Columbia Literary History of the United States* (New York: Columbia University Press) pp. 972–92.

128   "But are Things as We Think They Are?" *TLS*, no. 4410, 9–15 October, pp. 1104–5 (Review of *Time and Narrative* by Paul Ricoeur).

1988

129   "The Function of Rhetorical Study at the Present Time" in Engell, James and Perkins, David (eds), *Teaching Literature: What is Needed Now*, Harvard English Studies 15 (Cambridge: Harvard University Press) pp. 87–109.

130 "J. Hillis Miller and his Critics – A Reply", *PMLA* 103, no. 5, pp. 820–1.
131 "NB", *TLS*, no. 4446, 17–23 June, p. 676.
132 "Thomas Hardy, Jacques Derrida, et la 'dislocation des âmes'", *Confrontation, Cahiers* 19, pp. 155–66.
133 "Wallace Stevens", in Axelrod, Steven Gould and Deese, Helen (eds), *Critical Essays on Wallace Stevens* (Boston: G. K. Hall & Co.) pp. 77–83.

1989

134 "The Function of Literary Theory at the Present Time", in Cohen, Ralph (ed.), *The Future of Literary Theory* (New York: Routledge) pp. 102–11.
135 "'Hieroglyphical Truth' in *Sartor Resartus*: Carlyle and the Language of Parable", in Clubbe, John and Meckier, Jerome (eds), *Victorian Perspectives* (London: Macmillan) pp. 1–20.
136 "*Praeterita* and the Pathetic Fallacy", in McGann, Jerome (ed.), *Victorian Connections* (Charlottesville: University Press of Virginia) pp. 172–8.
137 "Prosopopoeia and *Praeterita*", in Lockridge, Laurence S.; Maynard, John; and Stone, Donald D. (eds), *Nineteenth Century Lives: Essays Presented to Jerome Hamilton Buckley* (Cambridge: Cambridge University Press) pp. 125–39.
138 "Prosopopoeia in Hardy and Stevens", in Butler, Lance St John (ed. and introd.), *Alternative Hardy* (London: Macmillan) pp. 110–27.

1990

139 *Tropes, Parables, Performatives* (London: Harvester Wheatsheaf) (forthcoming).
140 *Versions of Pygmalion* (Cambridge: Harvard University Press) pp. 251. 1991
141 *Victorian Subjects* (London: Harvester Wheatsheaf) (forthcoming).

142   *Theory Now and Then* (London: Harvester Wheatsheaf) (forthcoming).

Selected Reviews, Interviews and Discussions of J. Hillis Miller's Work:

1986

Moynihan, Robert, "J. Hillis Miller", *A Recent Imagining* (Hamden: The Shoestring Press) pp. 97–131.
Sanchez, Matilda, "Que es leer, un tema de pelea sobre la escritura", *Tiempo Argentino*, Cultura Sección, 5 January, p. 8.

1987

Leonard, George, "Hillis Miller Interview", *Magazine* 3, (Summer), pp. 46–7.
Salusinszky, Imre, "J. Hillis Miller", *Criticism in Society* (New York: Methuen) pp. 208–40.

1988

Berman, Art, "Deconstruction in America", *From the New Criticism to Deconstruction* (Urbana: University of Illinois Press) pp. 223–74.
Norris, Christopher, "Aesthetic Ideology and the Ethics of Reading: Miller and de Man", *Paul de Man* (New York: Routledge) pp. 102–24.
Wihl, Gary, "J. Hillis Miller, *The Ethics of Reading*", *Textual Practice* 2, no. 2 (Summer) pp. 295–306.
"Forum", *PMLA* 103, no. 5 (October) pp. 819–21.

"Intervista a Joseph Hillis Miller", *2000 Incontri* 2 (Agosto/
Settembre) pp. 14–15.
"J. Hillis Miller", in Jay, Gregory (ed.), *Modern American Critics
Since 1955*, Dictionary of Literary Biography 67 (Detroit: Gale
Research Company) pp. 221–31.

Index